The *Best* of MEMORY MAKERS

OUTSTANDING
SCRAPBOOK
PAGES

Elsie's Machine

My Great Aunt, Elsie, loved to sew, which was lucky since being one of the oldest girls in a family of 12 children, that was one of her responsibilities with in the family. Her father, William, bought this fiddle base Singer sewing machine (dated between 1875 - 1890) for his wife, Elizabeth. But as their family grew larger, Elizabeth passed the task of sewing on to her daughters. When Elsie died from influenza in 1918 at the age of 19, the sewing responsibilities were then taken over by my Grandmother, Edith, who kept the machine all these years and eventually passed it on to her own daughter.

Elsie May Roper
1899 - 1918

MEMORY
MAKERS
BOOKS

Executive Editor Kerry Arquette   **Founder** Michele Gerbrandt

Editor Kerry Arquette

Book Design Nick Nyffeler

Art Director Andrea Zocchi

Craft Editor Jodi Amidei

Art Acquisitions Editor Janetta Wieneke

Photographer Ken Trujillo

Contributing Photographers Jim Cambon (Cambon Photography), Liz Campanella, Carol Conway, Marc Creedon, Tara Cruz, Camilo DiLizia, Christina Dooley, Joyce Feil, Image Concepts, Brenda Martinez, Jennifer Reeves, MaryJo Regier, Radius Photography, Geoffrey Wheeler Photography

Contributing Writer Anne Wilbur

Editorial Support Emily Curry Hitchingham, MaryJo Regier, Dena Twinem

Contributing Memory Makers Masters Brandi Ginn, Diana Graham, Diana Hudson, Torrey Miller, Kelli Noto, Trudy Sigurdson

Title Page Art, Elsie's Machine by Trudy Sigurdson, Victoria, BC, Canada

Memory Makers® Best of Memory Makers *Outstanding Scrapbook Pages*

Published by Memory Makers Books, an imprint of F & W Publications, Inc.
12365 Huron Street, Suite 500, Denver, CO 80234
Phone 1-800-254-9124

First edition. Manufactured in Singapore

07 06 05 04 5 4 3 2

Library of Congress Cataloging-in-Publication Data

Outstanding scrapbook pages : 250 of the best pages and techniques from the world's #1
  scrapbooking magazine.
       p. cm.
    Includes bibliographical references and index.
    ISBN 1-892127-30-X
    1. Photographs--Conversation and restoration. 2. Photograph albums--Specimens. 3.
  Scrapbooks--Specimens. I. Title: At head of title: Best of Memory makers. II. Memory
  makers.

TR465.O89 2003
745.593--dc21

                                                    2003052714

Distributed to trade and art markets by
F & W Publications, Inc.
4700 East Galbraith Road, Cincinnati, OH 45236
Phone 1-800-289-0963

ISBN # 1-892127-30-X

Memory Makers Books is the home of *Memory Makers*, the scrapbook magazine
dedicated to educating and inspiring scrapbookers.
To subscribe, or for more information, call 1-800-366-6465.
Visit us on the Internet at www.memorymakersmagazine.com

This book belongs to

Special thanks to the editors whose skills and vision have been the driving force behind *Memory Makers* magazine over the years: Darlene D'Agostino, Pamela Frye, Erikia Ghumm, Kari Hansen-Daffin, Pam Klassen, Dawn Mabe, Lynda Meisner, Debbie Mock, Amy Partain, Shawna Rendon, Lydia Rueger, Anne Wilbur.

TABLE OF CONTENTS

INTRODUCTION

The Best of Memory Makers *Outstanding Scrapbook Pages* was conceived as a tribute to those scrapbookers who have invested their time and talent in the creation of scrapbook pages which they graciously shared with *Memory Makers* readers over the years. From the first issue of our magazine in 1996, through issue #37 seven years later, we have showcased scrapbook art that pushes the envelope creatively, defining new standards for the craft and stirring the heart.

The decision to create this book was far easier than the actual selection of pages to be included. All art featured in the magazine over the years has been special and therefore narrowing down the pages to a precious few was somewhat like asking a parent to choose a favorite child. It was a task too large for any one person, and so the selections were made through committee.

Staff members reviewed every page of every issue of *Memory Makers* magazine. The process sucked us into a flood of nostalgia. I remembered photographing our very first cover featuring two scrapbook pages set artfully among a pile of apples. I recalled wondering what I was going to do with all those apples when the shot was complete! I imagined I could still smell the flowers used on the cover of issue #2 and reflected on cherished friendships developed with creators of different pages. I recalled crying with a scrapbooker over the story behind her photos. I remembered watching an artist skillfully working on a detailed border…

Memory Makers staff voted on favorite scrapbook pages. It was a challenge to weigh the merits of an early page made back in the days when supplies were limited and scrapbookers were just beginning to explore the art form, with today's cutting-edge art. Selections were ultimately chosen based on a wide range of criteria: Did the page impact scrapbooking trends? Was an extraordinary technique applied? Were the photos exceptional? Was the journaling memorable? Was the page uniquely designed? Was there a special something about the page that made it stand out?

The experience in creating this book has been satisfying for all of us at Memory Makers. It has been a trip down Memory Lane. We invite those of you who walked this path with us throughout the years to enjoy this nostalgic look back over the shoulder. Your passion for the preservation of life's moments has contributed to this book. And it is your passion that will mold the future of scrapbooking just as the pages you share with us will ultimately mold the future of our magazine and books.

These outstanding pages are sure to inspire us all.

Enjoy!

Michele

Michele Gerbrandt

HISTORY OF MEMORY MAKERS MAGAZINE

May 1996
The first issue of *Memory Makers*, the very first scrapbook magazine—was mailed.

→

September 1996
The first full edition of *Memory Makers* mailed to 4,000 charter subscribers.

→

June 1997
Memory Makers moves out of Michele Gerbrandt's in-laws' basement and into an "official" office.

January 2001
Three separate *Memory Makers* special issue publications added per year.

December 2000
Memory Makers is the number-one selling scrapbook magazine in the U.S. as reported by news-stand distributors.

←

August 2000
Memory Makers' Michele Gerbrandt brings scrapbook-ing to TV with the show, "Do it Yourself Scrapbooking."

←

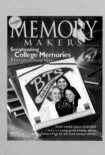

July 2001
Memory Makers is acquired by F&W Publications.

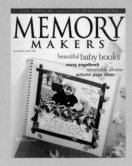

March 1998
Memory Makers hosts its first Croppin' Cruise.

September 1998
Memory Makers goes bimonthly, while also increasing the number of pages in each issue.

September 1998
Memory Makers publishes its first book, *Punch Your Art Out 1*.

March 2000
Memory Makers holds its first Page for the Cure contest to support the Susan G. Komen Breast Cancer Foundation.

June 1999
Memory Makers' receives 20,000th page idea submission.

July 2002
The first Camp Memory Makers is held in Grand Rapids, Michigan.

December 2002
Memory Makers is the number-one selling scrapbook magazine in the U.S. as reported by newsstand distributors.

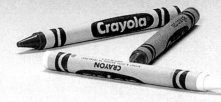

The Growing Up Years

WONDER flows from a child's face when she looks at the captivating world crying out to be explored and conquered. Wonder fills a parent's heart as she watches her babbling infant grow into a confident young adult ready to take on life's challenges. Photos that capture the world through a child's eyes and those that capture the child through her parents' are held forever on scrapbook pages. Whether vibrant as a playtime giggle or as subdued as a sleepy sigh, pages featuring children are sure to capture the uniqueness of the individual boy or girl and the unspeakable love of the parent.

INFANTS AND TODDLERS

Babies grow and change so rapidly that what once were vivid memories of baby's birth, toothless smiles, hesitant steps and babbling words quickly merge into a blurry montage of vague recollections.

Unforgettable baby pages bring moments from this foggy past into a sharp focus that clearly portrays the physical, emotional and spiritual facets of a young and cherished personality.

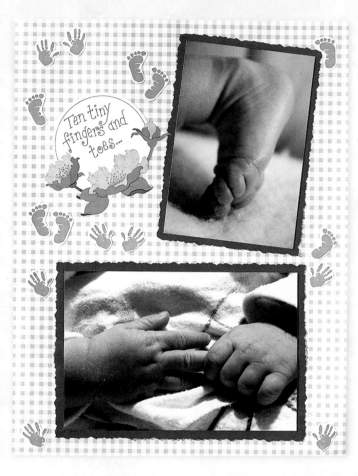

TEN TINY FINGERS AND TOES
September/October 1998
Issue #8
Kristi Hazelrigg, Washington, Oklahoma

Wanting to capture her daughter's pretty hands and feet, Kristi snapped these photos when her daughter Alison was just four months old. The black-and-white shots have a universal appeal to anyone who has experienced the wonder of little baby fingers and toes. Simple embellishment keeps the focus on the photos.

FIRST PORTRAIT
March/April 2003
Issue #35
Nicole Keller, Rio Hondo, Texas

An easy mosaic design, accomplished with square and flower punches, provides an appealing frame for this chalk-tinted newborn portrait. The soft pastel shades and patterns add both color and contemporary flair to the timeless appeal of the black-and-white photo.

BAYLEE ALEXANDRA
January/February 2001
Issue #22
Memory Makers
Idea inspired by Heather Coffin,
Spring Hill, Florida

Created in only a few minutes by die cutting a letter S into a specially folded sheet of paper, this intricate heart design is a stunning way to frame any photo. Heather Coffin of Spring Hill, Florida, discovered the technique while experimenting with a die-cutting machine. This interesting die-cut method is among many first introduced in the pages of *Memory Makers*.

OUR SNOW ANGEL
Holiday/Winter 1997
Issue #5
Joyce Feil, Golden, Colorado

The art of stained glass combines hundreds of glass pieces in a masterpiece of color and light that brilliantly glows within a framework of woven lead. Like many art forms, stained-glass concepts can be easily adapted to scrapbook layouts. This octagon design, inspired by a stained-glass pattern book, incorporates both a photo and complementary papers into its striking symmetrical arrangement.

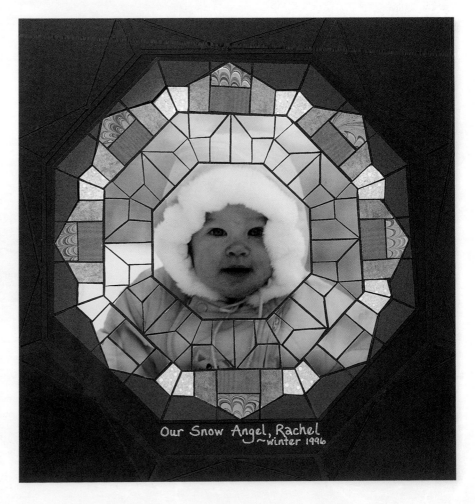

MEETING GRANDPA WEBB
May/June 2002
Issue #30
Tanya Webb, Tigard, Oregon

A monochromatic palette of soft yellows unifies this contemporary layout through various textures of handmade paper and black-and-white candids unconventionally tinted in the background. Wire accents and thorough computer journaling further accentuate the modern design. A photo enlargement, layered beneath computer-printed vellum, frames the same snapshot and provides perhaps the most dramatic yet subtle design element.

NATURAL WOMAN
November/December 2002
Issue #33
Anne Heyen, New Fairfield, Connecticut

Anne gave birth to her son Daniel after being told she could never get pregnant again. She says this Carole King song reflects not only her love for Daniel but also the Mother's Day photo taken "au naturel." Textural heart elements made from materials as varied as cork, raffia, jute and metal enhance a delightful mother-son love theme.

ME & MY DAD
January/February 2002
Issue #28
Memory Makers
Photos Diana Bolinger

Because the hand-tinted, deckle-edged photos look so authentically vintage, this page's calendar date at first glance prompts a double take. Complemented by 1950s stripes, plaids and solids, the father-son candids give the impression that Daddy just pulled into the driveway in his '57 Chevy and stopped on the front step to greet little Johnny. Whimsical title lettering and a paper-pieced hat fit the old-fashioned illusion.

CHILI PEPPER BABY
September/October 1999
Issue #14
Rebecca Hanson, Gilbert, Arizona

Photographer Anne Geddes has inspired perhaps millions of photos mimicking her famous shots of babies dressed as flowers, animals, insects, fruits and vegetables. Inspired by Geddes' imaginative scenes, this page combines silhouette-cropped Halloween photos, vivid die cuts and thin tan strips to create the illusion of a braided chili pepper garland. The contrast between the red and green draws the eye to the cherubic baby faces.

SPAGHETTI AND MEATBALLS
September/October 1998
Issue #8
Joanna Barr, Lowell, Michigan

Scalloped meatball photos tossed among piles of wavy noodles are the perfect recipe for this delicious page. Inspired by a baby's unforgettable spaghetti-smeared face, the cream-colored pasta provides both dimension and movement without overpowering the photos.

LITTLE YELLOW DUCK
September/October 1999
Issue #14
Cathie Allan, Edmonton, Alberta, Canada

Thin and delicate bubbles, simply stamped and cut out, not only provide a unifying design element but also fill this page with a sense of fun and adventure. Creative cropping and layering techniques lead the eye from the floating face near the upper edge down to the bubble-framed yellow duck and contented bath baby. Careful placement of the photos and paper-cut yellow duck reinforce this visual path.

6 MONTHS OLD
September/October 1998
Issue #8
Denise Bennett, Midland, Georgia

A little boy's energy, vitality and joy are mirrored in the bold colors and geometric shapes that surround these baby photos. The stained-glass design is simple to create by arranging matted photos on a dark background and filling in with colored triangles. One straight photo anchors the page while the remaining snapshots are placed askew for a sense of whimsy and movement.

NANCY & STEVIE MILLER
July/August 2000
Issue #19
Cheryl Thomas, Highland, California

A classic black page wallpapered with folk-art apples makes this appealing heritage portrait look like it could be hanging in Grandmother's kitchen. Creamy white milk and homemade cookies along with carefully arranged school-books further convey an all-American-kids theme, while simple lettering embellishments complete the old-fashioned country look.

FAMILY TRAITS
May/June 2002
Issue #30
Christina Chrushch, Rocky Mount, North Carolina

Family resemblances are strikingly apparent in this father-and-sons triptych created using photo edit-ing software. With five carefully selected paper mats, the black-and-white portraits stand out against a background of rich navy and maroon. Downloaded computer fonts, letter stickers and padded adhesive are other modern conveniences that contribute to the balanced design.

ABIGAIL 1936
Spring 1998
Issue #6
Memory Makers

Brass template embossing is one ideal solution for the perpetual scrapbooking problem of how to appropriately embellish heritage photos. The technique is easy enough for even a child to accomplish and requires only a light box, embossing template and stylus. The elegant tone-on-tone texture yields an almost irresistible temptation to rub the bumpy embossed surface.

1948
July/August 2000
Issue #19
Nadine Babbitt, San Diego, California

Nadine saved this lock of hair from her first haircut for about 50 years before encasing it on this page. Although the memorabilia pocket is modern, the retro lettering style, pink and black colors and checkerboard pattern instantly set the vintage photograph in its late 40s time-frame. The freehand-cut polka-dot bow and silver scissors add bold thematic elements. Even the black photo corners, here used as embellishments rather than to hold photos, recall the old-fashioned scrapbooks that might have previously held the vintage photo.

FLOWER GIRL
Spring 1998
Issue #6
Debbie Hewitt, Agoura, California

Just six black-and-white candids portray myriad facets of this captivating young personality—shy youth, giggling toddler, Daddy's girl or just a kid with an attitude. The simple border, woven from long wavy strips layered with floral stickers, accentuates the hand-tinted color and effectively frames the layout.

SUNMAID® SWEETHEART
March/April 1999
Issue #11
Johanna Large, Bloomington, Illinois

Although the raisin box held by Johanna's daughter was actually a bribe to get her to smile, it prompted this instantly recognizable design. The accurate rendition of the raisin box logo, lettering and colors imparts a sense of realism to the larger-than-life photo frame. Added details of the child's "net age" and personal journaling tell a sweet story.

HILTON BEACH
July/August 2000
Issue #19
Jenny Lowhar, Miami, Florida

A bold spiraling sun perched above an ocean painted with shades of blue raffia provide strong graphic elements to both complement and balance the vivid beach candid. The end result is an impressionistic effect that keeps the layout simple while adding both texture and dimension.

A LOOK BACK: *Scrapbooking With Paper Dolls*

In the beginning, there were paper and scissors, the main tools available to make paper dolls. By the spring of 2002, when *Memory Makers Creative Paper Dolls* special edition was published, the scrapbook market was bursting with an enormous variety of paper doll products. Die cuts, templates, preprinted dolls, patterns, computer software, paper-piecing kits, stickers and punches now make it easy to customize a paper doll to match the theme, colors and mood of any layout.

The fun of paper dolls encompasses not only the simple pleasure of dressing a human figure and adding details to create an individual personality. For scrapbookers, paper dolls also offer a universal language that can write a visual story about human activity, emotion and relationships. This versatility gives paper dolls an appeal that will far outlast any scrapbooking fad.

RAG DOLL
Winter 1997
Issue #2
Lorna Dee Christensen, Corvallis, Oregon

Simple pen work injects personality into a rag doll freehand cut and pieced from colored art paper. In addition to stitch lines on the clothing and highlights on the hair, two dots and a little round O are the perfect details to create a charming face. The old-fashioned figure brings life to the 1960s-era photos.

GIRLS DAY
January/February 1999
Issue #10
Jolene Keiko Wong, Monterrey, California

Adorned in colorful washi paper, abstract Japanese paper dolls stand with arms upraised to celebrate Girls' Day with a softly smiling maiden. The angelic poses of these abstract figures reflect her innocence and beauty, while their red kimonos convey a cultural message symbolizing the sun, vigor and good fortune.

FLOWER CHILD
March/April 2001
Issue #23
Barbra Otten, Durand, Michigan

Spring brightly blooms in a paper doll scene that replicates each element of a vivid Easter photo. The aged flower barrel bursts with pink tulips, the rosy-cheeked die-cut doll is dressed to match the curious toddler, and circle punches provide tiny toes for his pudgy bare feet. The scene effectively expands the world of the photo beyond its physical borders.

MARY KAY LADIES
March/April 2002
Issue #29
Kathleen Childers, Christiana, Tennessee

Readily available body and hair die cuts jump-start a paper doll design while leaving room for custom details. In this case, matching outfits and heavy makeup accentuate the humor of the beauty queen snapshots and faked business card.

SWING KID
March/April 2003
Issue #35
Joan Fowler, Kingston, Ontario, Canada

Wind rushes through curly blond locks swept up in a bright red ribbon, and pink legs reach higher with each forward arc. Were it not for tiny hands grasping taut steel chains, this paper doll might jump off the page during her fearless flight. A photo-traced pattern, curly doll's hair and jewelry chain contribute to the realism of a child swinging with joyful abandon.

BOYS

James Thurber understood the elusive nature of boys, from toddler to teenager and beyond, when he quipped, "Boys are beyond the range of anybody's sure understanding, at least when they are between the ages of 18 months and 90 years."

Indeed, boys both young and old often challenge scrapbookers to discover hidden facets of the masculine personality. Boy-theme pages that capture this sense of intrigue and mystery, like the proverbial diamond in the rough, reveal a brilliance of unique character.

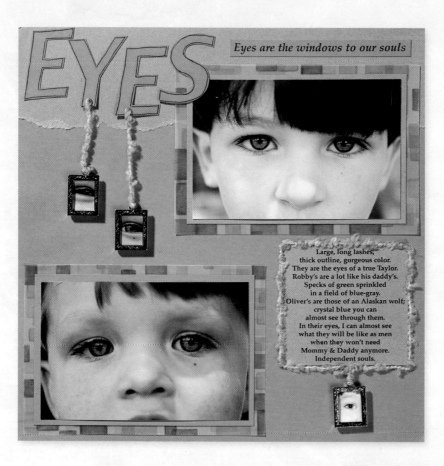

EYES
January/February 2003
Issue #34
Shannon Taylor, Bristol, Tennessee

A background of serene blues and greens pops these close-up photos of serious young eyes, while eloquent and detailed journaling shades them with heartfelt emotion. Tiny framed eyes suspended with nubby fiber complete a striking visual theme.

OVERALL
January/February 2003
Issue #34
Julie Labuszewski, Centennial, Colorado

Photographed from interesting viewpoints, black-and-white candids convey the independence of a little boy absorbed in his own private world. Denim embellishments hand-sewn to the page represent a favorite pair of overalls and inspire the witty title. Written from a mother's perspective, the journaling paints a charming personality portrait.

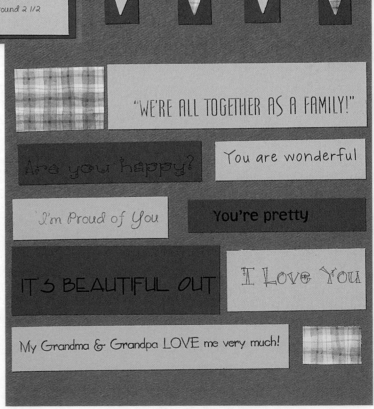

SENTIMENTAL SON
May/June 2002
Issue #30
Pam Lindahl, Chokio, Minnesota

Focusing on one aspect of a young son's personality, a bevy of decorative fonts repeat his sincerely uttered sentiments. A wavy plaid and shades of blue unify the color-blocked captions, folk-heart border and deco-style title. The photo embodies the down-home, country boy character of the layout.

RILEY
July/August 2003
Issue #37
Kelli Noto, Centennial, Colorado

A dog may be called "man's best friend" but any boy with a pooch will tell you that dogs are a "boy's" best friend as well. This delightful page captures the camaraderie between kids and their pets, drawing a bit of rough-and-tumble into the design with a burlap frame and mat, personalized dog tags and a link collar.

SWAMPED
July/August 2001
Issue #25
Colleen Macdonald, Calgary, Alberta, Canada

Recalling "memories of childhood filled with days spent searching muddy waters for creatures of the swamps," the poetic caption is also a graphic element representing the rushing water. Handcut reeds and cattails embellished with punched frogs and dragonflies grow tall next to the visually flowing words. The simple pleasures of youthful water explorations are forever preserved in jar-cropped photos capped with mulberry "plastic" and brown paper rubber bands.

There's nothing dreary about a rainy day...

when there are puddles to play in!!!

Isaac 1997 2 years old

RAINY DAY
Spring 1998
Issue #6
Tami Comstock, Pocatello, Idaho

Puddle-stomping sneakers pounding wet cement epitomize the carefree days of childhood when time passes slowly and even rainy days are bright. A grass-lined sidewalk converging toward the horizon pulls the eye toward the focal photo of an all-American youthful explorer.

BEAM OF SUNLIGHT
January/February 2002
Issue #28
Christina Chrushch, Rocky Mount, North Carolina

Monochromatic color blocks give the illusion that this dreamy black-and-white candid hangs in a bright window. As if the boy were gazing into his future, the textured color and thoughtful quote symbolize a sunny future filled with hope, potential and possibility.

A child is a beam of sunlight from the Infinite and Eternal, with possibilities of virtue and vice - but as yet unstained.

Lyman Abbott

NOAH'S ARK
September/October 2000
Issue #20
Susan Badgett, North Hills, California

In this amazing year-in-review layout, nestled among a menagerie of animals and photos floating in a paper ark atop swirling ocean waves, is an incredibly creative journaling block. Besides predictable facts such as favorite foods and best sports, also listed are unusual highlights including meanest idea ("cutting up my brother's Pokemon card"), best name drop ("Jesus told me I sleep with you"), bad habits ("blowfish marathons and loud burping") and profanity ("you hockey pockey"). These delightful details shape an unforgettable character vignette.

CHRIS
January/February 2000
Issue #16
Memory Makers

While names and other labels are usually secondary to the photos, this page reverses the typical scrapbooking order by making the journaling the focus and embellishing each letter with photos. The diagonally arranged photo letters, created using alphabet puzzle templates, contribute a sense of boyish energy, and leftover photo scraps frame the page with interesting and unexpected details.

FALL FRIENDS
September/October 2000
Issue #20
Memory Makers
Photos Charlotte Wilhite, Arlington, Texas

Based upon the designs of Frank Lloyd Wright, this page is itself a work of art. The circle photos are completely integrated into a geometric design composed almost entirely of intersecting arcs that energetically sweep across the page. Inspired by Arts & Crafts-era colors, the soft olives, tans and browns emphasize the fall time frame and complement the colors in the boy-and-his-dog photos.

PIZZA NIGHT
November/December 2000
Issue #21
Memory Makers
Photos Pennie Stutzman, Broomfield, Colorado

Paper-punched olives and handcut mushrooms and green peppers top a tasty page that pictures a Friday-night-pizza tradition. Surrounded by family candids, the clink of frosty mugs, steaming slices and eager fingers, a son's beaming smile conveys his simple satisfaction.

WATER FUN
July/August 1999
Issue #13
Charlotte Wilhite, Arlington, Texas

The title of this layout refers as much to its techniques as to its photos. The blue background painted with watery ink, fish-theme paper and stickers, photo-punched bubbles and splashy title letters all convey a sense of fun and excitement about a young boy's swimming accomplishments. An underwater disposable camera is the secret behind the interesting viewpoint of the enlarged photo.

PLAYGROUND FUN
July/August 2002
Issue #31
Linda Jernigen, Fairfield, Ohio

A chalk-shaded and pen-detailed playground is an ideal backdrop for the carefree joys of swishing down a sun-warmed slide, hanging from monkey bars and playing airplane tummy-side-down on a chain-link strap swing. Quickly created from a paper-piecing kit and embellished with contemporary sticker accents, the familiar equipment places the photos in a colorful and instantly recognizable context.

LUNCH BUNCH
September/October 1999
Issue #14
Julie Walkup, Silver Spring, Maryland

All it takes is a camera to compress a favorite lunch box into a scrapbook. The silhouetted bags and boxes tie in the "lunch bunch" theme and also reflect the stories and characters that influence contemporary children's culture—Toy Story, Barney, Disney, Dr. Seuss and Winnie the Pooh. For the title, photocopied letters of the child's own handwriting illustrate another creative use of memorabilia.

AT THE TRAIN DEPOT
July/August 2001
Issue #25
Susan Evans, Sparta, Tennessee

Photographed beside a classic luxury car, these modern boys dressed in argyle berets and elastic suspenders evoke the timelessness of a bygone era. The photo mats add a hint of fresh color, while the black photo corners and background confirm the old-fashioned theme.

SCHOOL PORTRAIT
September/October 1999
Issue #14
Barbara Miller, West Linn, Oregon

This school portrait page puts a youthful heritage photo in perspective by linking it to an activity that, at the time, was highly honored. More than casual journaling, the diploma reveals a facet of this child that would not otherwise be revealed. The combined elements of the photo, background paper and certificate speak in a united voice to reflect a simpler time when children took pride in and were recognized for their community service.

SMILE

January/February 2002
Issue #28
Christina Chrushch, Rocky Mount, North Carolina

It's not just the title that literally stands out on this page—the young man's charming grins are simply irresistible. Subtle tans and stripes keep the background neutral, and thin mats accent each page element with a touch of masculine red.

ALEX

July/August 2003
Issue #37
Trudy Sigurdson, Victoria, British Columbia, Canada

Dried flowers, leaves, charms, tiles, fibers, mesh, eyelets and other embellishments tell the story of a seek-and-find day at the lake. Right out of the pocket of the child and onto the page, this "shabby chic" grouping adds depth, color and texture to this all-boy design.

A LOOK BACK: *Scrapbook Journaling*

Penned in white ink on the black construction-paper pages of Grandma's old scrapbook, beside small black-and-white photos loosely held by lick-and-stick photo corners, are simple words describing people, places and events. Two generations later, written with an archival pigment pen on acid-free, lignin-free, buffered scrapbook pages, beside cropped color photos and elaborate embellishments, are surprisingly similar captions.

Times have changed, but even in a modern world of sophisticated computer fonts, decorative lettering templates, myriad pen colors and letter punches, die cuts and stickers, the fundamental value of the written word has not changed. Today's scrapbook pages still reflect the understanding that without words, photos eventually become meaningless. While retaining this core value, modern scrapbookers have also taken the words of their scrapbooks to an entirely new level in terms of both content and creativity.

DREAMS FOR SARA
September/October 1998
Issue #8
Kim Owens, Lynnwood, Washington

Complete sentences aren't always necessary to convey an eloquent message. In this simple design, a mother uses single words to communicate her dreams and hopes of the things she wants her child to have and become. Colored blocks provide visual pauses that punctuate the verbal paths around each photo.

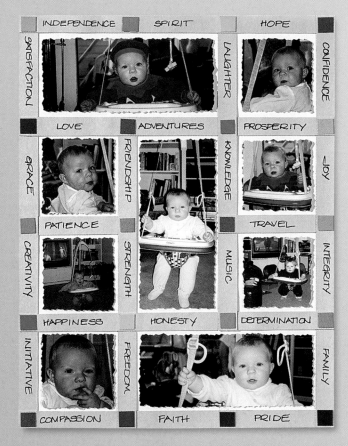

WACKY WORLD
March/April 1999
Issue #11
Melissa Evans, Lyons, Kansas

Everyday objects can inspire creative writing as well as page design. This board-game concept offers an intuitive journaling style that combines photo facts with play instructions. The captions verbally connect a dozen miscellaneous photos into an appealing design that reads in a clockwise fashion.

OUR FAMILY CIRCUS
March/April 1999
Issue #11
Helen Rumph, Las Vegas, Nevada

Look no further than the Sunday comics for both design and journaling inspiration. The familiar format makes it easy to illustrate any story, especially humorous anecdotes. Although the dialogue bubbles require few words, along with the images they accomplish the same goals as any great story—setting the scene, introducing characters, developing a plot and achieving a resolution, in this case, a punch line.

REMEMBER WHEN
September/October 2002
Issue #32
Andrea Steed, Rochester, Minnesota

Word pictures are an ideal way to include unphotographed memories in a scrapbook. The short stories on this layout illustrate that bringing these memories to life doesn't require a lot of verbiage. Just the simple facts are enough for the reader to shape a mental picture of the people and events. A variety of fonts printed on sheer vellum provides an interesting presentation.

What a season Alec had! Alec was jumping out of his skin for this season to begin. He practiced and practiced to get a chance to **pitch** and finally Dad thought he was good enough to try it out in a game. Alec pitched great for his first time! He STRUCK SEVERAL PLAYERS OUT and ended up pitching for 5 innings his first game pitching. Although he was a very good pitcher it certainly wasn't his best position. Most of the season he spent at **short-stop**.

But towards the end of the season he got a try at **catcher**. We think he has fallen in love with this position. Of course, the catcher's equipment was his favorite part, but he loved everything to do with this position. He was VERY GOOD AND HAD VERY FEW MISSED BALLS. He found out very quickly that it was a hot position though! (The equipment does have its disadvantages!) Alec had a great season **hitting** as well. He ended the season with a ·538 BATTING AVERAGE and HIT 2 IN-THE-PARK HOMERUNS! He was the ONLY ONE on the team to hit an in-the-park home run so he was pretty proud. Alec was chosen to try-out for the 9-10 year old ALL-STARS TEAM and had a very good try-out. This year he wasn't chosen to be part of the team so he has his sights set on next year.

Little League

LITTLE LEAGUE
March/April 2003
Issue #35
Donna Downey, Huntersville, North Carolina
Photos Debbie Krekel, Burlington, Iowa

Energetic computer fonts both emphasize the highlights of a boy's memorable Little League season and imbue the newspaper-style caption with movement and action. This journaling style requires only a basic knowledge of word-processing software and keeps the details of the season as fresh as the images.

ALIKE, DIFFERENT
May/June 2002
Issue #30
Kelli Noto, Centennial, Colorado

When writer's block strikes, sometimes the best remedy is to pose a question or reflect upon a theme. Pondering the similarities and differences of her children helped this mother to both write about and photograph her sons from a unique perspective. The page idea is further reinforced by the flip-flopped, color-blocked page design.

Alike...

Different...

UNIQUE
March/April 2003
Issue #35
Pam Easley, Bentonia, Mississippi

Although scrapbookers invest huge quantities of time, energy and love in their family chronicles, they often forget to include information about themselves. Through words and photos of favorite people, places and things, this layout brings the often-invisible family historian to the forefront and tells her story through the ambitious use of more than 100 fonts. Photos layered beneath vellum windows and elegant leaf embellishments weave visual elements into the list of vivid phrases.

GIRLS

"There was a little girl who had a little curl, right in the middle of her forehead. When she was good, she was very, very good, but when she was bad she was horrid." Henry Wadsworth Longfellow's humorous reflection on the nature of little girls adds a dose of reality to the pithy "sugar and spice, and all that's nice" nursery rhyme.

Perhaps he understood, like many scrapbookers, that girls are a study in contrasts. Shy and outgoing, crying and giggling, or tough and tender can all describe a young girl, sometimes within the same ten minutes. Scrapbook pages that understand these contrasts convey the essence of a uniquely feminine individual without need of cliché.

KENZIE

July/August 1999
Issue #13
Linda Strauss, Provo, Utah

Strong summer shadows filter through tree branches, casting golden patches of warmth onto a young girl lost in the pleasure of a kitten's soft fur. The organic title letters, spelled with dried grasses and flowers, echo the outdoor theme.

WHY GOD MADE LITTLE GIRLS
May/June 2002
Issue #30
Sheila Boehmert, Island Lake, Illinois

Straw hats, plastic beads, silk flowers and gowns bring wide smiles of delight to young girls absorbed in the make-believe lives of princesses and brides. The black-and-white photos ingeniously eliminate any clashing colors, allowing the pink and lavender palette to dominate. Ruffled mats, stamped dress-up accessories and a long strand of pearls tie up the feminine theme.

STRAW HAT
July/August 2000
Issue #19
Oksanna Pope, Los Gatos, California

Emerging from clusters of pale green leaves, lavender buds and blooms reach upward, drawing the eye toward the warm and vivid photo of the girl on the beach. Created with nonwrinkling paper paint and a sponge stamp set, the wildflowers reflect the child's natural beauty.

WALK TOGETHER
March/April 2003
Issue #35
Annie Wheatcraft, Frankfort, Kentucky

Big-brother and little-sister feet pause on a spring carpet of pink petals, suggesting the side-by-side companionship they may share. As if to illustrate the moral directive of the page, diverse elements such as Scrabble tiles, plastic buttons, metal mesh, shiny brads, painted eyelets, colored chalk, stamping inks and hand-sewn letters peacefully coexist in an eclectic and textured title.

JESSICA & POOH
Summer 1998
Issue #7
Memory Makers
Photo Tonya Jeppson, Boise, Idaho

Like a vivid hummingbird frozen in mid-air, a girl and her bear pause in their swinging, suspended by taut tan ropes that stretch their imagined ties to strong honeysuckle vines. Soft blossoms swirl around the breezy blue background, softly sketched with colored pencils and oil pastels.

LAZY SUMMER DAYS
January/February 2003
Issue #34
Trudy Sigurdson, Victoria, British Columbia, Canada

Layered between torn paper sand dunes, masses of thin strips imitate the wind-blown beach grass in the sandy portraits. The title flap lifts up to reveal a detailed caption and the remaining title nestled among additional layers of sand and grass. The grass provides such a striking textural element that little additional embellishment is required.

LITTLE GIRLS
September/October 2000
Issue #20
Linda Astuto, Amarillo, Texas

A towering tree bursting with brown crayon branches and vibrantly water-colored leaves dwarfs a happily swinging child. Her diminutive appearance in relation to the tree as well as the blond hair and pink clothing perfectly illustrate both "little" and "girl." The juxtaposition of the tiny realistic photo against the grandiose painted backdrop reinforces the fairy-tale mood of a familiar poem.

OH BEAUTIFUL FALL
September/October 2002
Issue #32
Erikia Ghumm, Brighton, Colorado
Photo Cheryl Rooney, Lakewood, Colorado

Simple stamping techniques tint this page with lush autumn color. Pressing a leaf stamp onto an inked block stamp yields the unusual reverse-image designs in the mosaic frame. A square block stamp provides the soft diamond shapes behind the title and captions. The warm red and green inks pull the colors in the brother-and-sister photo to the forefront.

CAYRA
March/April 2000
Issue #17
Deidre Tansey, Smithers, British Columbia, Canada

How is a child like a color? Penned from an affectionate mother's perspective, four color-coded captions offer poignant and poetic answers to this question. Like many "accidental" inspirations, the page theme was sparked by indecision about which mat color to select. The resulting layout provides verbal and visual insights into a bright and bubbly feminine personality.

KELLIE
January/February 2003
Issue #34
Jodi Amidei, Lafayette, Colorado
Photo Leslie Aldridge, Broomfield, Colorado

A sunny spring day and the equally sunny smile of a little girl are paired perfectly with the refreshing hues of coordinating patterned paper arranged in this photo-flattering style. As if pulled straight from her own jewelry box, delicately strung beads suspend the qualities this child embodies. Torn vellum, additional bead accents, and a heartfelt caption create a softness that makes this page a lovely and loving tribute.

AYSHA AND I
May/June 2003
Issue #36
Trudy Sigurdson, Victoria, British Colombia, Canada

Broken mirror chips bode anything but bad luck for this beautiful mother/daughter page. Chips are added to tags, decorated with dried flowers and wrapped with decorative wire. The journaling block includes ragged chip-shaped boxes which highlight important words and add power to the heartfelt text.

My name is Kylie.

I can count to 20.

I know my ABC's.

I love to sing and dance.

I read books to Ma-Ma.

I like paints, markers and scissors.

I love to swing.

I love jumping on the "trampopine".

This is a picture of my funky hair.

My Pa-pa thinks I'm Little Miss Einstein.

Little Miss EINSTEIN

LITTLE MISS EINSTEIN
March/April 2002
Issue #29
Deb Lyle, Elida, Ohio

When a static-charged trampoline session stood a young brunette's hair on end, her grandmother was poised and ready. The humorous photo prompted the scientific theme personalized with self-descriptive journaling written from the girl's perspective. The specific, concrete elements that describe her abilities and preferences help capture the essence of her individuality.

Cutest little pumpkin in the patch!

Nora and I watched this pumpkin grow all summer. Nora picked it, and I put it on the front porch. When we got home that night it was smashed in the street. I'm so glad I took this picture!

CUTEST LITTLE PUMPKIN
September/October 2000
Issue #20
Karen Regep Glover, Grosse Point Woods, Michigan

Plump pumpkins, mini checks and pleasing plaids provide a softly patterned background that balances the vibrance of the grinning gardener. Diagonally mounting a photo mat is a simple technique that adds a sense of movement. The soft greens represent the idea of youth and nature, while the oranges stimulate the page with energy and warmth, suggesting the change of season.

FRIENDS FOR LIFE
September/October 2000
Issue #20
Adrienne Lubbe, Highway Gardens, South Africa

Soaring paper-cut trunks branch into spring blossoms, growing summer leaves, golden autumn color and bare winter boughs. The visual analogy pictures the seasons of life represented in the photos of lifelong friends taken 35 years apart. The symmetry of design mirrors the parallels between the photo pairs.

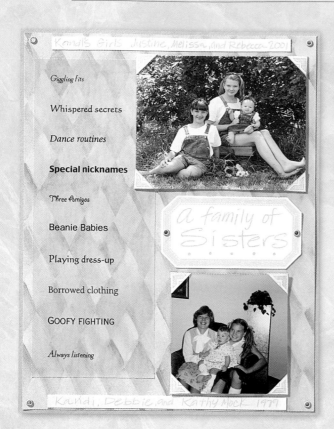

A FAMILY OF SISTERS
May/June 2002
Issue #30
Erikia Ghumm, Brighton, Colorado
Photos Debbie Mock, Denver, Colorado

A young Debbie Mock (*Memory Makers* editor) is wearing pigtails in the bottom photo, while her three nieces pose in the contemporary black-and-white portrait. The page draws attention to the striking similarities and describes with two-word, poetic phrases the universal experiences that sisters often share.

THE JOY OF SISTERS
May/June 2001
Issue #24
Teri Vokus, Sarasota, Florida

Little about the love and bond between sisters needs articulating beyond that which can be seen in their smiles when together. This connection is exemplified by the telling title and understated design of this page. Utilizing only minimal sticker embellishments and a string of selected sentiments, it incorporates childhood photos alongside a more recently captured moment, creating a sense of nostalgia. It speaks to the timelessness and transcendence that is sisterhood.

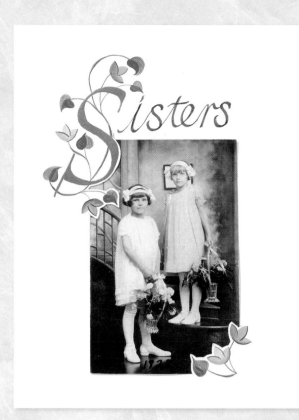

SISTERS
Spring 1998
Issue #6
Memory Makers

Reminiscent of old European manuscripts, illuminated letters are an easy and elegant way to embellish any page, and modern materials make this medieval art form accessible to crafters of all levels. Here, a single gold character intertwined with watercolored flowers gracefully frames a 1928 heritage photo. Tucking the photo beneath slits cut around the illuminated letter and flowers eliminates the need for permanent mounting.

LOCKS OF LOVE
September/October 2001
Issue #26
Tish Michel, Reedsburg, Wisconsin

This layout is one of many inspiring entries in the Page for the Cure™ contest, an annual event that *Memory Makers* originated in 2000 to raise money for the Susan G. Komen Breast Cancer Foundation. In this prize-winning spread, shades of blue, pink and purple paper unify elements as diverse as photocopied newspaper articles, an event logo, candid photos, a formal portrait and a certificate. These elements cohesively present the story of a girl's remarkable act of generosity.

Stephanie taking picture in the mirror

Camera Ready,
Aim,
Shoot!

Stephanie Age 3

Budding
Photographer

BUDDING PHOTOGRAPHER
January/February 2002
Issue #28
Debra Beagle, Milton, Tennessee

Putting a camera in a child's hands is an easy
way for snapshot photographers to include
themselves in their own scrapbooks. This layout
not only unfolds the humorous story of a little
girl's first picture-taking attempts but also
depicts a loving mother-daughter relationship.
Soft lavenders lend a feminine touch to support
simple twisted-wire flowers.

A
little
crooked.
Try again.

Smile!

August 2000
You were so cute this day,
wanting to use Mommy's camera.
You have this love for photography
and scrapbooking, just like
Mommy. I am so proud of
these pictures you took of
me. At 3½ you exhibit so many
talents. I love you so very much
and I am so proud of you.

Perfect!
Mommy Age 33

Rachel's Favorites

Animal ·	Kitty's & Pony's
Color ·	Yellow & Pink
Drink ·	Root Beer & Hot Chocolate
Food ·	Pizza & Mac&Cheese
Fruit ·	Apples & Red Grapes
Vegetable ·	Carrots
Worst Food ·	Mustard
Candy·	Taffy & Gum
Toys ·	Barbie's & Dolls
Movie ·	Sleeping Beauty
Play·	Grocery Store
Dance ·	Jazz & HipHop
Singers ·	Brittany Spears & Christina
Group·	NSYNC
TV Channel ·	Disney
Store ·	San Rio "Hello Kitty"
Loves·	Being Tickled
Hobbies ·	Dancing, Singing, Dress-Up, Sledding, Swimming, Playing with her friends and little brother, Coloring, Doing Mommy's Hair Listening to music, Piggyback Rides, Pillow Fights With Uncles.
Friends ·	Kaitlin, Ella & Jeremy Jasmine, Anna, Megan, Allie, Samantha, Jessica, Chase, Daniel, Anna I. and Rachel T.
Places to go ·	To the Pool & last But not least Great America

Daughter
She's a little bit of sunshine,
She's a smile to light your days,
She will steal your heart and
Keep it warm with her endearing ways,
She's your precious little daughter,
With a sweetness from above
Who fills your years with laughter
And your lives with Lots of Love.

RACHEL
March/April 2002
Issue #29
Sheila Boehmert, Island lake, Illinois

Feathery paper and beautifully stamped roses give these black-and-white portraits the special treatment they deserve. A detailed list of favorites sketches a word portrait to accompany the strong visual images of her ear-to-ear smiles. Pink embroidery floss hand-stitched around the edges further softens the mood.

BARBIE GIRL
November/December 2002
Issue #33
Sheila Boehmert, Island Lake, Illinois

Wriggling long vinyl legs into a fashionable heart-print evening gown, pulling thin spaghetti straps over smooth white shoulders and slipping miniature high-heels on pointy feet are just the beginning of Barbie playtime joys. A well-equipped dollhouse is just the ticket once Barbie is all dressed up with no place to go. These photos visually document Barbie-gear details that can be enjoyed by even a grown-up Barbie girl.

Stephanie, Rachel and George have been friends since they were 2. Now they are 11 - almost 12 - and they all have braces! George's are green, Rachel's are green and purple, and Stephanie has blue. But next week they could be pink and orange.

HEAVY METAL GANG

September/October 2001

Issue #26

Karen Regep Glover, Grosse Pointe Woods, Michigan

Unbendable friendships are cemented by shared experiences such as metal braces with colored bands. The lettering style lends a sense of electricity and excitement, while tooth die cuts wrapped in thin gray strips support the clever title.

IT'S HIP TO ZIP

March/April 2003

Issue #35

Diana Hudson, Bakersfield, California

From a head-hugging microphone and fake-fur-trimmed tank top to hot pink tiger-print pants, dangling chain link belt and shiny black zip-up shoes, this modern girl epitomizes the universal appeal of dress-up play. Black paper, clear shrink film and a machine-sewn zipper replicate the look of the vinyl boots, while pink brads and metal vellum tags provide additional page hardware. A pull-out caption recalling fond memories of childhood go-go boots further defines the experience.

It's hip to zip

Priceless

Sydney
7 years old

A girl can never have too many shoes. These boots were absolutely irresistible. We had to have them... and I say WE because my favorite shoes when I was a little girl were some white go-go boots. Besides, they match the outfit! Isn't playing dress-up FUN!

BIRTHDAY parties, weddings, anniversaries, holidays and other celebrations make up the high points of our lives. They are often the milestones that mark progress; yardsticks that measure growth. Photos are as much a part of celebrations as laughter and hugs. These captured events find a home on scrapbook pages to be enjoyed again and again. From gift-openings to flag wavings, to feasting and wild costumes, holidays and other kick-up-your-heels events create bright and beautiful, pastel and peaceful scrapbook memories.

LOVE YOU MOMENTS

Celebrations that commemorate relationships which are treasured and revered are some of the most significant of all. Valentine's Day, weddings, prom, Mother's Day and other special times speak loudly about the importance of sharing what we carry in our hearts.

FOREVER AND ALWAYS

July/August 2003

Issue #37

Pamela Frye, Denver, Colorado

Nothing captures the color of love quite like rich, deep hues of red and pink as those used in this page. Utilizing two different fonts and sizes for this tender title creates special emphasis, as does the artfully framed caption of sweet sentiments. Glossy embellishments, torn paper, and intricate borders whimsically offset the classic look and romantic feel of the black-and-white photograph, making this page an elegantly executed labor of love.

BE MINE

January/February 2001

Issue #22

Rebecca Sower, Springfield, Tennessee

Hearts of all styles—swirly, asymmetrical, angular or traditional—harmonize with mother-child Valentine's Day photos. A paper appliqué pattern played in shades of red, white and tan is the time-saving design secret. Like a visual love song, the layout sincerely voices a mother's perspective on the meaning of a traditional holiday.

HAPPY HEARTS
January/February 2001
Issue #22
Teresa Villanueva, Aurora, Colorado

Freeform red hearts accent simple silhouettes of a celebratory figure, blooming flower, stately tree and outstretched hand. A church brochure designed by Sally Beck inspired the contemporary appliqué designs in this quilt-style Valentine's page. The symmetrical arrangement pulls the eye toward the central title and theme.

BRINLEY
January/February 2003
Issue #34
Brandi Ginn, Lafayette, Colorado

Fishing in a continuous stream of new scrapbook products, *Memory Makers* reels in the best catch of innovative tools and techniques, including many that save valuable scrapbooking time. Here, a photo mat quickly colored with a cube-shaped texture stamp accents a coy smile. Realistic eyelet stickers that appear to hold the title and caption in place eliminate the need for setting eyelets with special tools. The dimensional hearts are precut shrink-plastic charms that require only heat. Created in minutes, these contemporary elements delightfully enhance the cheesy and charming grins.

1946 WEDDING
Autumn 1996
Issue #1
Memory Makers
Photo Karen Gerbrandt, Broomfield, Colorado

Antique white, handcut vines and layered flowers entwined around a simple gray frame typify the "less is more" principle that applies to heritage page designs. The restrained use of color and embellishment allows the photo to remain the focus.

FIFTY GOLDEN YEARS
January/February 2000
Issue #16
Terry Van Ryn, Littleton, Colorado

A 50th-anniversary party portrait is lovingly embraced with an intricate embossed paper frame. Burgundy and gold, the colors chosen for the celebration, are carried through on this page and others in Terry's album, matching the golden anniversary theme.

BRIDE & GROOM
Spring 1997
Issue #3
Sandi Genovese for Ellison Craft & Design, Lake Forest, California

Miniature doves, hearts and butterflies die cut from creamy white art paper encircle a 1920s wedding portrait with symbols of love and fidelity. Straight-pin piercing supplies detail, dimension and texture.

IMAGINE
May/June 2003
Issue #36
Amy Madzinski, Naperville, Illinois

"The sun was shining brightly and there was but one cloud in the sky," writes Amy of her wedding day. Her face shines with the faith and joy she feels about her new beginning as a wife. Vellum covers much of the page and poetic tags on a bead bracelet are the perfect accessory for a perfect wedding.

THEY SAY IT'S JUST A SISTER THING
May/June 2003
Issue #36
Jody Jackson, Parmelee, South Dakota

Sisters will be sisters, whether dressed up in bridal attire or dressed down in jeans and sweatshirts. Even in the midst of a formal occasion, these two sisters share the sillies as well as deep affection. A journaled vellum block overlays a photo of pillars; stamped and embossed ferns support the elegance of the wedding.

ENCHANTÉ
May/June 2003
Issue #36
Jeanne Ciolli, Dove Canyon, California

A prom memory should be golden, a message Jeanne Ciolli underlined with her glittering treatment commemorating her son's prom experience. Gold embossing powder and paper-pieced roses evoke a romantic evening while details of the "who's" and "where's" are detailed in a journaling block and on the invitation which has been included as a design element on the page.

OUR WEDDING
July/August 2002
Issue #25
Michelle Minken, Littleton, Colorado

Heritage papers, borders and sticker embellishments lend an old-fashioned feel to a new union. This simple but elegant page was created in less than 20 minutes without compromising beauty. Minimal journaling, simply matted photos and coordinating corner accents tie the elements together beautifully.

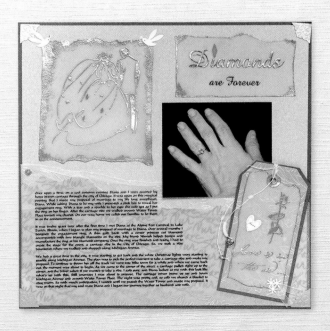

DIAMONDS
May/June 2003
Issue #36
Diana Graham, Barrington, Illinois

A moonlight carriage ride, sparkling Christmas lights and a marriage proposal from the man she loved marked the beginning of engagement for Diana Graham. The perfect ring topped a never-to-be forgotten evening. The magic of that night is recorded forever on this page embellished with diamond-like mirrors, metallic papers, fibers, a charm and romantic heart, dove and flower stickers.

WEDDING RING QUILT
Spring 1997
Issue #3
Marie-Dominique Gambini, Lyon, France

A color-copied quilt sewn with traditional Provençal fabrics frames a young couple with the patterns and colors of their French heritage. The dark-colored outer wedding ring symbolizes eternal love and unity, while the light-colored inner arches pull the eye toward the central photo. With the symmetry, balance, colors and patterns built into the quilt, cutting out the inner frame was the sole design requirement for this page.

TO HAVE AND TO HOLD
January/February 2000
Issue #16
Sarah Fishburn, Fort Collins, Colorado
Photo Lorna Dee Christensen, Corvallis, Oregon

Layered on white paper between thin strips of black "leading," asymmetric rectangles of colored vellum achieve a luminous stained-glass effect. The design bathes the page with color and light without overwhelming the vintage wedding portraits. Silver lettering communicates key details with elegant style.

WEDDING CAKE
May/June 1999
Issue #12

Eileen Ruscetta, Westminster, Colorado
Photos Party Crashers, Littleton, Colorado

Traditional cake-cutting festivities inspire each design element in an elegant and energetic wedding layout. Meticulously pieced from photo scraps, a mosaic border ties in both the lattice backdrop and photo colors. Photo-realistic flower stickers adorn a paper-pieced replica of the three-tiered wedding cake. Burgundy paper accentuates the silhouetted cake masterpiece and pair of entwined hearts. Matted business cards even give credit to a skilled cake decorator.

OUR FLOWER GIRLS
May/June 2001
Issue #24

Matt Corwin, Lacoochee, Florida
Photos Jolita Rishel, Pasadena, Florida

Wreathed in a bouquet of blossoms, these flower girls beam from a frame of sticker art. Companies, such as Mrs. Grossman's, make intricate sticker designs possible by producing stickers which are mirror images. These stickers can be set down in simple patterns to produce less-than-simple results. Minimal journaling keeps the focus on the frame and those fresh flowers within.

FAMILY TRADITIONS

Christmas, Chanukah, Thanksgiving, Easter and other yearly holidays hold some of the most cherished memories of both our early years and adulthoods. They symbolize a coming together of family and friends, and each time traditions are repeated they become richer and more important. The sharing of these occasions are truly gifts.

WHITE CHRISTMAS
November/December 1999
Issue #15
Susan Sigle, Pretty Prairie, Kansas

A background of deep navy and black immediately brings vintage wintry photos to center stage. Rich evergreen holly leaves, circle-punched berries and stamped-and-embossed snowflakes provide subtle embellishment. The Gothic-style lettering, handcut using a template, gives equal presence to the titles and captions.

GLAD TIDINGS
November/December 2001
Issue #21
Memory Makers
Inspired by Nancy Castaldo, Chatham, New York

On this 8½ x 11" page, 16 tiny greeting cards burst out of a translucent vellum envelope. Reducing the images on a color copier is the ingenious technique that eliminates holiday card clutter while still providing a way to enjoy the colorful photos and images.

HOLLY WREATH
November/December 2001
Issue #21
Nanette Morone, El Cajon, California

Realistically highlighted with pencil and a gold pen, a fluffy red bow crowns a holly wreath that features 20 photos and over 30 handcut holly leaves. Corrugated paper and two shades of evergreen impart a sense of depth and texture. Circle-punched berries provide additional splashes of color.

CHRISTMAS TREE
Holiday/Winter 1997
Issue #5
Joyce Feil, Golden, Colorado

Like giant, fluffy snowflakes, punched and doodled hearts flutter down a colorful Christmas page. The windy caption swirls around a die-cut tree frame, whistling a familiar holiday tune. Strips and triangles of festive paper border the happy tree-hunting theme.

AS GOOD AS GOLD
November/December 2002
Issue #33
Sheila Boehmert, Island Lake, Illinois

Modern supplies and technology simplify this golden Christmas layout. Printed on vellum with an ink-jet printer and immediately heat-embossed with gold powder, the title and captions match the shimmering ribbon mats. Contemporary gold and silver patterned vellum wrap up beribboned holiday packages, and prepackaged tree and ornament embellishments require only peel-and-stick mounting.

CHRISTMAS 1999
November/December 2002
Issue #33
Kate Nelson, Fountain, Colorado

An Internet idea inspired hand-sewn Christmas trees decorated with button ornaments. Stitched with only a needle and fiber, the trunks and branches enhance the simple folk-art appeal but keep the focus on the family portrait.

ADVENT CALENDAR
November/December 1998
Issue #9
Memory Makers

As shown in this cheerful Advent calendar, creative scrapbooks can pass down holiday traditions as well as hold family memories. First created in the 19th century, Advent calendars originally contained Scriptures or drawings of biblical scenes to help teach children about the meaning of Christmas. Constructing a modern version is easy using the pattern in the original issue. The fun for scrapbookers is designing 24 tiny scenes using stickers, die cuts, small photos, captions and other embellishments. The fun for children is the excitement and anticipation of a personalized Christmas countdown.

CHANUKAH
Holiday/Winter 1997
Issue #5
Randi Green, Woodland Hills, California

Photographic candles add personal meaning to a traditional menorah. Smudged with a cotton ball, yellow ink adds a warm glow to each flame. Die-cut letters simply proclaim the holiday.

CHANUKAH
November/December 1998
Issue #9
Memory Makers
Photos Kerry Arquette, Arvada, Colorado

Inspired by the concept of an Advent calendar, each candle in this paper menorah opens like a door to reveal a photo or religious symbol. Connecting a visual triangle with a dove and Star of David, a simple flowing prayer captures the essence of the Feast of Lights.

FIRST HANUKKAH
November/December 2002
Issue #33
Melissa Ackerman, Princeton, New Jersey

Perched on an embossed gold menorah, nine candles softly glow behind a vellum caption describing a young girl's delight with a new baby doll. Shades of purple enhance the photo and tie in the lavender title. For the outer border, thin mitered strips give the full-page matting effect while saving cardstock.

KWANZAA
November/December 2002
Issue #33
Amy Gustafson for Hot Off the Press, Canby, Oregon

Candles in symbolic colors shed light on the Swahili words for the seven principles of Kwanzaa. The tribal-inspired lines and patterns in the border, photo mat and title letters reflect the celebration of African heritage.

NEW YEARS EVE
January/February 2003
Issue #34
Tricia Morris for Club Scrap, Greenville, Wisconsin

The elegant, contemporary tags on this New Year's layout illustrate one of many stamping techniques that have migrated from the stamping world into the pages of creative scrapbooks. Created with simple stamping and embossing, the double-sided tags are held in place with wire and eyelets so they are visible from both sides of the page. The tags provide an interesting textural embellishment that unifies both the paper and photo colors.

THANKSGIVING 2000
November/December 2001
Issue #27
Maria Loomis, Anacortes, Washington

A spectacular montage of autumn leaves and corn owes its impact to pigment ink and clear embossing powder. The background actually began as a sheet of ivory paper first stamped and heat embossed with clear ink and powder. Rubbing over the clear embossed images with shades of pigment ink brought them "to the surface." Additional leaves and corn stamped in black and a final clear embossing finished the shiny, almost enameled surface. The custom look reflects the fun of stamping techniques as much as Thanksgiving joviality.

WE HAVE SO MUCH
November/December 2001
Issue #21
Memory Makers
Photo Amy Giacomelli, Monrovia, California

Printed paper scraps blended in an autumn-theme collage warmly enhance a Thanksgiving family portrait. The touch of blue marbled paper plays off the earth tones to keep the page from feeling too heavy. Paper-punched birch leaves accentuate the leaf motif, and seasonal stickers tie in the season and family theme.

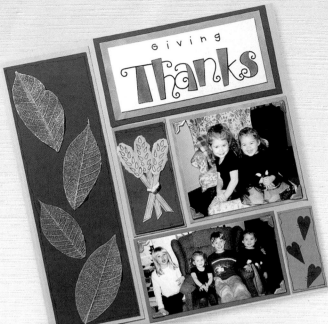

GIVING THANKS
November/December 2001
Issue #27
Peggy Kangas, Pepperell, Massachusetts

Emblems of autumn including wheat bundles, crimson leaves, ripe acorns and plump corn fill the spaces around young-cousin candids. Paper-piecing patterns make quick work of the cut and torn designs embellished with simple pen strokes. Stylized lettering colored with suede paper draws attention to the theme, while gold photo corners and lacy leaves add sparkle and shimmer.

GRANDMA'S PIE
November/December 1999
Issue #15
Susan Badgett, North Hills, California

Coconut, lemon, peach, boysenberry, apple, chocolate, banana cream, cherry, pecan— pies in myriad flavors served on a delectable holiday wreath give literal meaning to "fruitful labor." Stamped pine needles spice up the background for circle-punched and silhouette-cropped lemons, apples and bananas. With shiny flatware stickers, this page is set and ready to serve.

A LOOK BACK: *Creative Photo Cropping*

Cropping, which is the process of cutting photos to enhance the image or eliminate portions of the shot, is the original creative scrapbooking technique that requires only photos and a pair of scissors. When the scrapbook market exploded in the late 1990s, so did the variety and availability of cropping tools, including decorative scissors and rulers, shape templates and cutters, die-cut machines, corner and shape punches, cutting mats and specialty craft knives.

As illustrated in countless scrapbook layouts and in *Memory Makers Creative Photo Cropping for Scrapbooks,* published in 2001, the ideas for creative cropping are as limitless as the photos themselves. Sometimes a photo itself dictates the need for cropping to remove a busy background, to eliminate photo imperfections or to improve a photo's focus. But any photo, other than historic, artistic or Polaroid photos, can be cropped simply to add style and variety or to create a unique work of art.

TEA SIPPING COUSINS
Winter 1997
Issue #2
Joyce Feil, Golden, Colorado

With pinkies delicately extended, beribboned and hat-clad young ladies sip grown-up pleasures if only for a moment before running off to play. Silhouette cropping suggests an imaginary Anne-Geddes-style world of giant red teacups filled with delightful young faces.

HANGING OUT TO DRY
Autumn 1997
Issue #4
Pat Brookes, Bonita, California

A thin clothesline laden with sleepers, socks, overalls and pants hangs from colossal, towering sunflowers. Cropped entirely from extra photos and interesting scraps, the photomontage integrates mismatched snapshots into a cohesive, fairy-tale-like scene. Generous documentation describes grandson joys and mishaps.

ROLLIN' ROLLIN' ROLLIN'
October 1998
Issue #8
Eve Lowey, Newport Coast, California

A series of baby-rolling-over photos shot in rapid succession show that creative photography often precedes creative cropping. Partial silhouetting and layering produces a motion-picture effect. The title and wavy border further emphasize the movement.

GARDEN MOSAIC
May/June 1999
Issue #12
Sandra de St. Croix, St. Albert, Alberta, Canada

Photo mosaics are an inviting technique that require only a few photos and an accurate paper trimmer, a simple square punch, or a mosaic template—whatever the favorite tool. Here the mosaic technique connects photos of a Canadian garden in full bloom, preserving the vivid colors for year-round enjoyment. Thin white spaces between the squares allow the eyes to rest as they peacefully wander from bloom to bloom.

WATER SKIING

July/August 1999
Issue # 13
Barbara Wegener, La Quinta, California

An enormous enlargement makes it easy to see the details of a young water skier leaning into the wake, gripping a pull rope to stay afloat. The smaller photos are cropped and placed to blend into the water-filled scene. Each successive image adds another detail to the adventure.

1998

January/February 2000
Issue #16
Mette Harding, Burke, Virginia

From springtime tree climbs and summer beach balls to autumn hikes in the woods and holiday festivities, these jumbo-sized numbers pack in a year of memories. Photos are silhouette cropped and carefully layered so that each number appears to be cut from a single photo. The background fills in the details with a summary of the year's highlights.

PUMPKIN HARVEST
September/October 2000
Issue #20
Memory Makers
Photos Sandra Escobedo, Manteca, California
Inspired by Hallie Schram, Billings, Montana

Understanding of both dimension and light are necessary to create intricate three-dimensional illusions. Photos are cropped to fit preordained spaces. Lighter photos are mounted on lighter blocks, while darker photos are mounted on darker paper. Continuity is the key to carrying off this complex pattern of cropped crates.

TAKE IN THE WONDER
January/February 2003
Issue #34
Julie Labuszewski, Centennial, Colorado

A barefoot walk along the beach gains a sense of movement from sliced and staggered photo edges. The simple cropping technique adds visual interest to balance the emotional impact of the artist-authored poem. A swirly sun stamp and hand-sewn sun rays fill extra space with subtle texture.

SUNDAY BEST
March/April 2002
Issue #29
Sandy Brown, Forest Grove, Oregon

Streaming Easter sunshine basks four angelic children with bright background light, painting a golden halo above each smiling face. Pale shades of tan, pink and green pull the sunlight into the old-fashioned layout. Mimicking the look of vintage wallpaper, the damask background perfectly matches the antique settee. Delicately chalked velveteen hats adorned with punched and torn flowers make the ultimate fashion statement for this dressed-up layout.

EASTER EGG HUNT
March/April 2002
Issue #29
Nancy Finch, Orlando, Florida

Pastel solids and plaids draw attention to a vivid photo of two explorers absorbed in the magic of a traditional Easter event. Dressed to match his photo counterpart, a die-cut egg hunter proudly displays a basket filled with punched eggs and paper grass. Lavender tulips bloom in each title letter, announcing the page with style.

NICOLE & ISABEL
March/April 2000
Issue #17
Memory Makers

A soft and fuzzy page literally makes an impression with the use of velvet stamping. Originally developed for reverse-embossing on real velvet, this technique works on velvet scrapbook paper using an iron and an inked or uninked rubber stamp. This soft and tactile background combines three basic designs and several shades of ink to enhance a cheerful Easter photo.

EASTER ATTRACTIONS
March/April 2000
Issue #17
Susan Badgett, North Hills, California

A deckle-cut sun peeps behind grassy green hills teaming with a drove of ink-smudged, cotton-tailed bunnies that almost seem to wriggle with excitement. Framed with striped stickers and woven ribbon, the warm and energetic layout beautifully integrates a dozen Easter photos as well as extensive, personalized journaling in a cohesive and fun-filled spring romp.

MOTHER'S DAY
May/June 2001
Issue #24
Stacey Shigaya, Denver, Colorado
Photos Connie Mieden Cox, Westminster, Colorado

Humorous or serious, witty or sentimental, top-ten lists provide an easy template for creative journaling that is both enjoyable to write and read. In this Mother's Day layout, ten pull-out captions offer personal meaning to 10 photos taken across the decades. Lovely pansies unify the diverse elements, and a soft and leafy background complements the feminine theme.

GOOD TIMES

Nineteenth-century zoologist Thomas Henry Huxley philosophized, "The secret of genius is to carry the spirit of childhood into maturity." Retaining the spirit of childhood is also the secret to the best birthday celebrations, whether for a country or individual. Fireworks, flag waving, hot dogs on the grill, ice-cream cake, helium balloons and, most important, family and friends, are the high points that mark these annual celebrations.

2000
July/August 2001
Issue #25
Cathie Allan, Edmonton, Alberta, Canada

Stamped paper strips laced through diagonal photo slits literally weave hopes and dreams around a proud graduate. The lines move upward and outward, conveying a sense of expanding horizons and a future exploding with limitless possibility. Festive balloons and folksy stars add to the sense of celebration.

MAY YOU HAVE JOY
May/June 2003
Issue #36
Gayla Feachen, Irving, Texas

Diplomas made from rolled and corded pieces of paper and gold embossed mortarboard stamps add just the right touch of ceremony to this graduation page. The journaled quote speaks as eloquently as any commencement speaker to a young graduate whose face beams with excitement at the thought of embarking on life's adventures.

May you have joy on this your graduation day. Always have a sense of how unique you are. Never doubt how much you have to give. Have faith in your abilities. Follow your dreams in every day you live.

A Look Back: *Scrapbook Kaleidoscopes*

Peering through a kaleidoscope reveals a world of patterns and colors spinning and collapsing into each other. Peering into a scrapbook reveals the colors and patterns of life. When Judy Nurkkala of Bloomington, Minnesota, visualized a way to blend the two, her idea took the concept of photo art to a new level. The March/April 1999 edition of *Memory Makers* introduced her concept of cutting original and reverse-image photos into geometric angles and piecing them together to mimic the kaleidoscope's beautiful form and effect.

Memory Makers Photo Kaleidoscopes, also published in 1999, develops the technique in detail, including how to select a photo, obtain reprints, cut photo angles and assemble the cut pieces. Although photo kaleidoscopes may look complicated, the 350 entries in the May/June 2000 *Memory Makers* photo kaleidoscope contest attest to the fact that anyone can replicate the fascinating patterns, forms, movement, lines and colors.

Our Vacation at the Beach
July/August 2000
Issue #19
Ashley Smith, Richardson, Texas

Against an intense blue sky, blazing sun rays emanate from a classic eight-piece photo kaleidoscope fashioned out of 45° pie shapes with silhouetted outer edges. The center spins like a swirling whirlpool. To complement the water theme, a fan-shaped kaleidoscope layered from six duplicate photos suggests a rushing ocean wave. Both kaleidoscopes merge in an interconnected layout of sky, sunshine and water.

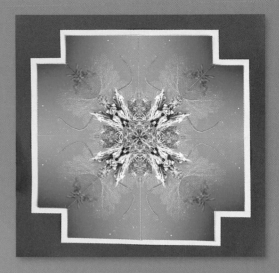

ALL AMERICAN BOY
May/June 2000
Issue #18
Florence Davis, Winter Haven, Florida

Photos with repetitive patterns, intersecting lines, vivid colors and good light quality produce the most dramatic kaleidoscope effects. The photo in this eight-piece kaleidoscope fits all of these requirements with a linear deck fence, angular stars and stripes, bright hues and soft light. The center begins with an exquisite burst of summer blooms merging into a ring of fence spindles and solid brown railing. In the distinct outer layer, vivid flagpoles and pale green grass form a pleasing starburst pattern.

UNDERWATER JEWELS
May/June 2000
Issue #18
Linda Casali, Livermore, California

An exotic, eight-tentacled sea creature seems to glide through a murky blue ocean in this eight-piece kaleidoscope. Made from an underwater photo, the seascape kaleidoscope contains incredible detail and organic beauty.

COWBOY TYLER
May/June 2000
Issue #18
Dorthy Rohner, Albany, Oregon

Armed with a rope and a mega-caliber grin, this little cowboy supplied just the bang needed for a complex kaleidoscope page. Dorthy's artwork took the grand prize in *Memory Makers'* photo kaleidoscope contest.

FALL KALEIDOSCOPE
November/December 1999
Issue #15
Terah Brossart, Spokane, Washington

Celebrating the season with its own colorful confetti, a joyful leaf-pile jumper tosses crunchy autumn leaves. Small maple leaves punched from printed paper seem to fly off the corners, while large photo-punched leaves add a lacy effect around the outer edges. The stamped saying not only sums up the page but also disguises the center opening in the eight-way kaleidoscope.

GOD BLESS AMERICA

July/August 1999

Issue #13

Teresa Ramirez, San Diego, California

A red, white and blue country patchwork celebrates all things American with familiar icons such as ripe watermelon, deep-dish apple pie, crackling firecrackers, gingham hearts and a folk-art flag. Inspired by a tole painting pattern book, paper dolls dressed in polka dots, checks and plaids brighten the layout with quaint personality. Black pen stitching and a loosely swirled star border round out the design.

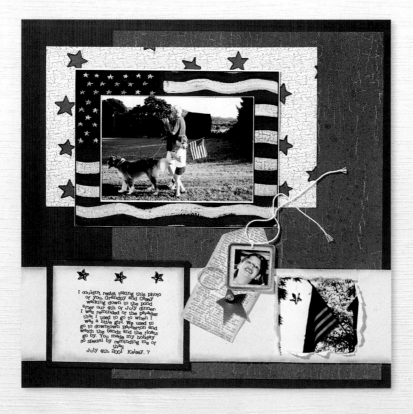

JULY 4TH

July/August 2003

Issue #37

Chris Douglas, Rochester, Ohio

Break out the band and strike up your favorite I Love America rendition, this special page will fit right in with weathered shades of red, white and blue and a heritage undertone. A star charm, glass bauble and photo are mounted on a tag which defines "freedom" in a multitude of ways. A gently ripped photo window and thoughtful journaling complete the story.

USA
July/August 2003
Issue #37

Shauna Berglund-Immel, for Hot Off The Press, Beaverton, Oregon
Photo Theresa Cutts, Portland, Oregon

This red, white and blue page rings with patriotism from sea to shining sea. Beads, charms and fibers add dimension to coordinating patterned papers. Tags and stitching supply a home-sewn, homemade feeling while showcasing this darling Liberty Belle.

THE GOOD OLD DAYS
July/August 2002
Issue #31

Mendy Mitrani, The Woodlands, Texas

Textured backgrounds and muted mat colors echo the old-fashioned, Americana look of button-adorned, knotted and corrugated page elements. The embellishments including the heart, stars, flag, corners and antique-white captions are preprinted and ready to cut out, saving considerable scrapbooking time. Letter stickers further simplify the title lettering. Raffia bows hide unwanted dates on hand-tinted contemporary photos of an antique Ford truck.

HALLOWEEN
November/December 1999
Issue #15
Kristi Hazelrigg, Washington, Oklahoma

Scattered strands of straw raffia, plump orange pumpkins and golden-hued autumn leaves frame an unforgettable "don't-mess-with-me" toddler face. Her deadpan expression and piercing blue eyes humorously contrast with a jolly dressed-to-match scarecrow and cheerful punch-art turkey. The caption, which slips behind the portrait to reveal the hand-lettered title, provides essential who, what, when and where details.

SPIDER WEB
September/October 2000
Issue #20
Donna Pittard, Kingwood, Texas

Happy trick-or-treating memories are woven into an artistically spiraled web handcut from a single sheet of white paper. The white lines against a black background direct the eye in a counter-clockwise motion from the smallest photo in the top right around to the bottom caption and focal photos. Created with swirl and circle punches, hot pink and purple spiders curiously survey the seasonal scenes with bright and bulging eyes.

HALLOWEEN
September/October 2002
Issue #32
Kathleen Childers, Christiana, Tennessee

Inspired by Halloween symbols and spooky legends, miniature punch-art vignettes tell tiny stories of haunted houses, menacing jack-o-lanterns, creepy cats, green-faced monsters, boiling cauldrons, hovering ghosts and rattling bones. The texture and pattern of Magic Mesh, hand-sewn raffia and checkerboard paper visually unify the layout.

HALLOWEEN
September/October 2002
Issue #32
Pam Kuhn, Bryan, Ohio

Using a square punch to crop and mat the focal point of each pumpkin-carving photo puts double prints to good use. Navy mats further emphasize the punched photo squares and add dimension to the full-size photos. The orange, tan and green color scheme ties in the organic theme through green raffia, ivy and floral patterns and real pumpkin seeds. Cut and photocopied newspaper fonts form a whimsical title.

LITTLE PUMPKIN
November/December 2000
Issue #21
Sandy Holly, Laguna Hills, California

This little pumpkin is the pick of the patch when featured on an eye-catchingly crisp fall page. Paper-pieced vellum forms a canopy of autumn leaves above her head and wind-blown leaves that frame the photo. Intricate paper piercing adds visual interest.

IT'S A PARTY
July/August 2002
Issue #31
Brandi Ginn, Lafayette, Colorado
Lettering inspired by Tara Cowper, Portland, Oregon

Craft wire, sun and balloon punches and raffia help write the "Party Time" letters for this festive birthday page. In the confetti-strewn border, embroidery floss ties up pretty packages and quilling strips add dimension to paper party horns. Polka-dot paper and torn edges enhance the sense of celebration.

HAPPY BIRTHDAY
July/August 2002
Issue #31
Joy Carey, Visalia, Calfornia

Painted with watercolors on a single sheet of tan paper, soft background colors complement the vintage look of sepia-toned birthday photos. Mary-Engelbreit-inspired checkerboards outline eight different design blocks that include photos, captions and hand-painted designs. The yellow sun, twinkling stars and candle flame add just a touch of bright color.

MY BIRTHDAY
March/April 2001
Issue #23
Julie Labuszewski, Centennial, Colorado

Similar to spoken words voiced longer or louder, written journaling can emphasize words and phrases with different colors and lettering styles. In this ball-laden birthday page, colorful pens jazz up the title and key words, spreading color throughout the page. A tiny chocolate muffin, pizza slice, tape measure, balloon, overalls and moon illustrate important elements of a fun-filled celebration.

BIRTHDAY BOWS
July/August 2002
Issue #31
Frances Goldwasser Reed, Atlanta, Georgia

A young girl's beaming smile warms an old-fashioned floral background bordered by piles of pretty presents. A well-arranged blue bow almost seems to rest atop her golden tresses. Thin strips of paper curled around a pencil add a festive touch of confetti, and an antique postcard folds back to reveal a detailed caption.

PARTY TIME
July/August 2002
Issue #31
Melissa Caligiuri, Winter Park, Florida

Sweet as the icing on Connor's birthday cake, this bright page draws its color scheme from lemony star stickers. Party hats and corner accents were created to complement the festive mood of a first birthday celebration. While the birthday boy will grow older each passing year, the page design is timeless.

A LOOK BACK: *Scrapbook Paper Tearing*

Paper piecings, borders and other embellishments take on a whole new form when shapes are torn instead of cut. Perfect for outdoorsy or playful layouts, designs can look rugged, soft or whimsical. The beauty of this technique comes from its imperfections, so mistakes only add character. As further illustrated and explained in *Memory Makers Creative Paper Techniques for Scrapbooks*, published in 2002, paper tearing also offers a decorative edge that softens the look of any page element.

Perhaps because anyone can tear paper, the technique has an enduring appeal that provides surprising and spontaneous results depending upon the paper's texture, thickness and direction of the tear. The act of tearing is as satisfying as its delightful results.

DESERT BLOOM
Spring 1998
Issue #6
Pat Thuman, Scottsdale, Arizona

Simply torn mountains contribute soft texture to a serene landscape border. A die-cut cactus and sun complete the peaceful scene.

SECOND TO NONE
March/April 2000
Issue #17
Linda Strauss, Provo, Utah

An orange basketball soars toward a backboard in the hopes of swooshing through its woven net. Combined with photos placed askew, the angles of the pen-detailed design heighten the sense of movement and action. An energetic poem tells a story of "swishes, sweat, the ball, the net" with the compelling enthusiasm of a proud parent.

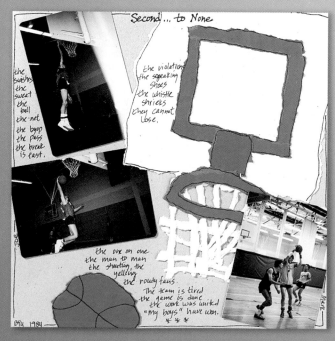

I Love Books
September/October 2000
Issue #20
Missy Rice, Whittier, California

A "cubby little tubby all stuffed with fluff" as well as a "very hungry caterpillar" prompted these whimsical illustrations of favorite book titles. The paper-torn designs recall the pleasures of many cozy reading sessions.

Two by Two
September/October 2000
Issue #20
Linda Strauss, Provo, Utah

A giant-sized Noah complete with beard, robes, staff and sandals seems to hold up this framed photo of a sunny day at the zoo. Thin paper wisps not only nestle the messenger dove but also humorously depict a balding patriarch.

When I was 4
July/August 2000
Issue #19
Memory Makers
Photo Christina Hutchinson, Corona, California

With visions of plump gray mice scurrying in their heads, two fancy felines purr contentedly in the corner of this cuddly page. Torn paper provides the "purrfect" technique for suggesting fur's soft texture.

BEYOND your front yard, down the block, around the corner, throughout the nation and across the seas, the wide world calls. It is rich and ripe with nature, with adventure and growth. Whether gardening, dreaming, vacationing or otherwise interacting with the outdoors, spectacular photos are waiting to be taken and placed on album pages that tell the story of journeys beyond your front door.

SUMMER

When Shakespeare said that "summer's lease hath all too short a date," he probably wasn't thinking of pool parties and seaside vacations. But his observation still holds true—three months seem altogether inadequate to fully enjoy lazy days filled with sunny relaxation and recreation.

Summer pages, however, like a glass of fresh lemonade, squeeze photos and words into memorable refreshment that still tastes sweet when summer's blooms have long faded.

ON THE SEASHORE
July/August 2001
Issue #25
Memory Makers
Photos Sandra Escobedo, Manteca, California

Muddy feet and sandy toes peep from a textural background woven with freeform, wavy strips. The intense combination of aqua and orange ties in the water and sunshine, and the wavy title and captions further develop a sense of movement.

UNDER THE SEA
January/February 1999
Issue #10
Sandy Holly, Laguna Hills, California

In the hands of a scrapbooker, a good sharp craft knife is like an artist's paintbrush. Here, a fish design freehand cut from a single sheet of blue paper simulates the look of intricate stained glass. The technique creates a focal point with both texture and design interest.

Boys and Girls of Summer

March/April 2002

Issue #29

Marie Hazzard, Springfield, Pennsylvania

A deco-inspired beach layout dresses up with artistically bent, twisted and bead-adorned wire elements. The tag-style captions do double duty by holding the wire in place as well as identifying young faces in the bright and sandy photos. A variety of computer fonts contribute to the sense of whimsy, while pink and blue highlight the title and theme.

GARDEN AT THE CABIN
May/June 1999
Issue #12
Linda Schell, North Vancouver,
British Columbia, Canada

Like a hidden-pictures game, close examination is required to find the spotted butterflies, spinning spider, slithering snake and croaking bullfrog that blend into the upper collage of summer garden photos. A graceful arbor cut from a sheet of stationery draws attention to prized daylilies. The lower page re-creates a lovely climbing clematis with heart, sun and spiral punches.

JAKE & BLAKE
November/December 2002
Issue #33
Kelly Angard, Highlands Ranch, Colorado

The colors, patterns and textures of summer find their way into a mosaic frame pieced from cropping leftovers. The design expands the glimmering photo of two boys by a pond and breaks up the rectangular theme with dynamic triangles and diagonals.

LAZY DAYS
July/August 2002
Issue #31
Oksanna Pope, Los Gatos, California

Hand-knotted with beige embroidery floss, a miniature hammock swings from summer trees laden with punched green leaves. The scene envelops the pages with a sense of cool breezes and restful undulation, suggesting the peace and serenity of hammock snuggles.

AT THE BEACH
July/August 2000
Issue #19
Susan Walker, Oakbrook Terrace, Illinois

Hand-tinted photos match the soft colors of stencil-cut starfish, scallops and
tulip shells gently floating at the page bottom. Sheets of cream paper add
subtle background warmth.

ENDLESS SUMMERS
January/February 2003
Issue #34
Torrey Miller, Thornton, Colorado

Like foggy memories, vellum symbolically fades these
heritage photos, while oval windows let viewers peer at
long-ago summertime faces. Connected with brass
chains against a colored background, stamped and
embossed copper suns light up a sharp, contemporary
present in contrast to a blurry, black-and-white past.

DREAMING OF THE LAZY DAYS OF SUMMER

January/February 2003
Issue #34
Kelli Noto, Centennial, Colorado

A sensitive touch and an artistic eye managed to combine this dreamy photo of brothers engaging frogs and dragonflies in a too-blue-to-be-real pond with cartoon-like clip art. Mulberry paper adds texture for reeds and cattails, while a butterfly sticker flutters, drawing the eye toward the title. This layout manages to be both cool as pond water and warm as a mother's hug.

SUMMER VACATION

July/August 1999
Issue #13
Donna Leicht, Appleton, Wisconsin

Almost randomly scattered photo scraps sliced into strips and triangles convey the energetic movement of beach play as well as the dominant theme of sky and sand. Angular, color-coded lettering matches the jagged and triangular theme. On the facing page, fabric squares recycled from a favorite pair of shorts add further geometric embellishment.

FAVORITE THINGS
March/April 2002
Issue #29
Lisa Hanson, Hudson, Wisconsin

A simple color-blocking technique finds fresh texture with printed vellum layered over pale green rectangles and hand-stitched, zigzag borders. The wavy photo mat complements the design of the shiny embroidery floss, suggesting the movement of rolling waves. Shaded fill-in lettering draws attention to the strong focal photo of a grandmother and grandchild.

LEGACY OF LOVE
May/June 2003
Issue #36
Cathie Allan, Edmonton, Alberta, Canada
Photos Marie-Dominique Gambini, Lyon, France

Stamped flowers and leaves create a background of restful color for a lattice-framed garden of fresh summer photos. Flower eyelets add texture as well as attach additional foliage to the layout. Pull-out captions identify photo subjects with creative style.

STATE CHAMP
March/April 2000
Issue #17
Linda Strauss, Provo, Utah

A bushy-tailed, beret-headed, bow-bearing fox struts across a layout honoring a young state archery champion. Pressed leaves grow from a paper-torn and pen-detailed tree trunk, and tiny punched flowers bloom at the roots. Interview-style journaling lets the champion humbly state his accomplishments.

YELLOWSTONE
July/August 1999
Issue #13
Hallie Schram, Billings, Montana

Evocative of the eerie, natural beauty of our nation's first national park, a soft pastel sunset glows warmly against a thick forest of dark evergreens. Blended with texture and tree stamps, the background brings color to these 1930s-era photos without undue distraction.

A LOOK BACK: *Scrapbook Punch Art*

When the fourth issue of *Memory Makers* introduced the concept of combining simple punched shapes to create captivating art-work, punch-art fever rapidly spread in the scrapbooking and paper-crafting world.

Based on the concept that all things consist of basic shapes, punch art combines these shapes into clever designs that take on a life of their own, adding charm and whimsy to scrapbook pages.

FRUITS AND VEGETABLES
May/June 1999
Issue #12
Marilyn Garner, San Diego, California

Furrowed with torn brown strips, fertile garden soil yields plump watermelons, lacy-topped carrots, red ripe strawberries, bright yellow sunflowers, spreading pumpkin vines and luscious lavender egg-plants. The punch-art produce grows around labeled seed packets sprouting colorful photos and even more punch-art designs. Printed paper and creative letter-ing plant further country charm in a well-staked layout.

PUMPKIN FEST
September/October 2000
Issue #20
Donna Pittard, Kingwood, Texas

Ripe and rustling ears of corn incorporate photos, journaling and punch art into one unified design. Punched ovals, cut in half and meticulously layered, form each ear of Indian corn. Careful penwork provides effective detail for each leaf and stalk. Even the photo mats are inked around the edges to blend with the overall design.

CHRISTMAS 1964
November/December 2002
Issue #33
LauraLinda Rudy, Markham, Ontario, Canada

The key to punch art is discovering new ways to use punched shapes. These whimsical elf hats with flannel edges are ingeniously created with a super giant contemporary tree punch paired with holly punches. The remaining elf features incorporate oval, teardrop, flower and circle punches. Painted with gel pens and colored chalk, each elf's expression matches the corresponding toddler in the photo. Although a dedicated mother's subway trip to Eaton's department store took its toll on the three young Santa sitters, the photo captures reality with small children much better than perfect smiles.

LAVENDER
January/February 2002
Issue #28
Véronique Grasset, Ruy-Montceau, France

Lavender, the symbol of the Provence region in France where it is widely grown, weaves a delicate border around captivating black-and-white candids. Hand-cut leaves and stems complement blossoms layered with punched and halved purple hearts.

TIANA AND TRAVIS
September/October 2002
Issue #32
Pamela Frye, Denver, Colorado
Photo Shawna Rendon, Westminster, Colorado

While not actually mounted on the page, punched leaves contribute to these tone-on-tone leaf blocks. The technique involves placing a punched leaf on an inked block stamp and then stamping onto scrap paper. When the leaf is removed and discarded and the image is stamped again onto green paper, the result is softly silhouetted leaves.

FALL

"Autumn is a second spring when every leaf is a flower," observed French writer Albert Camus. His poetic description identifies the visual appeal of a season when color again explodes in nature, transforming green foliage into ever-changing hues of yellow, gold, orange and crimson. Autumn scrapbook pages reflect this visual transformation as well as other seasonal sights, sounds, tastes and textures.

PARC DE LA TÊTE D'OR (GOLDEN HEAD PARK)
May/June 2003
Issue #36

Cathie Allan, Edmonton, Alberta, Canada
Photos Marie-Dominique Gambini, Lyon, France

A single stamp and various shades of embossing powder add color and dimension to lovely maple leaves layered behind day-at-the-park photos. Purple, green, yellow and rust papers enhance the lush autumn feel. Smaller than the photo dimensions, stamped and matted frames draw attention to each family grouping.

FALL
September/October 2002
Issue #32

Chris Peters, Hasbrouck Heights, New Jersey

Copper gusts scatter photo-punched oak leaves across a windy layout. Color blocking with warm autumn tones balances the freeform wire swirls. Laser die cuts and template lettering on a torn black border anchor the leaf-pile candids.

I love to photograph old buildings from different views

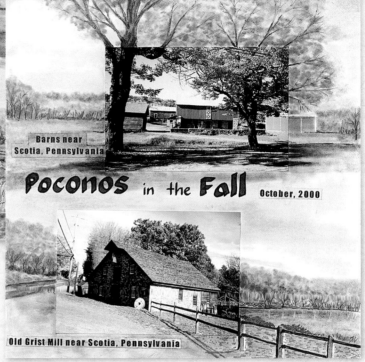

Barns near Scotia, Pennsylvania

Poconos in the Fall   October, 2000

Old Grist Mill near Scotia, Pennsylvania

POCONOS IN THE FALL

January/February 2003
Issue #34

Joan Reynolds, Derwood, Maryland

Artful chalk drawing enlarges the world of a scenic photo without a trip to the photo lab. The photo-extension technique creates one-of-a-kind panoramas with a breathtaking sense of expansiveness and beauty.

THE ART OF MARRIAGE

May/June 2002
Issue #30

Diana Graham, Barrington, Illinois

Die-cut leaves set above and below vellum create a romantic flavor for this couple's fall jaunt. While color choices and minimal embellishments add visual interest, it is the photos that captivate. Careful cropping and matting draw the viewer's eye to the subjects, with the same intimacy with which they view each other.

FISHING AT THE RIVER
January/February 2002
Issue #28
Nancee Testa, Fort Collins, Colorado

Black-and-white photos are coupled beautifully with colorful fall snapshots on this unusual page. A simple matting treatment using calm blues and greens ties the cropped images together. Branch and leaf stickers strategically placed along the page edge add a striking touch of both color and drama.

OCTOBER 2000
September/October 2001
Issue #26
Ruth Mason, Columbus, Ohio

Dimensional leaves that appear to hold each photo are created using the art of paper relief. The technique makes flat objects appear dimensional by shaping them with the back of a spoon and adding detail with dry embossing techniques. Careful layering and mounting further enhance the effect.

I love living in Minnesota because the changing of seasons is so distinctive here. And by looking at these pictures, it's easy to see why I like spending so much time at the lake.

A Picture Perfect Fall
September/October 1999
Issue #14
Terri Robichon, Hawick, Minnesota

Carefully hung on a striped sage "wall," seven photos depict the glory of a Minnesota fall and reflect a love of nature and family. Hand-drawn picture hangers and gray shading augment the realism of each framed image.

AMAZING ADVENTURE
September/October 2002
Issue #32
Kathleen Childers, Christiana, Tennessee

A sublime fall day, warm and full of color, inspired an autumn layout that incorporates photos, detailed journaling, beautiful color and homemade paper. Machine-stitched to the background, sage and rust pockets conceal pull-out strips with additional photos. The upper right photo card folds back to reveal a detailed, vellum-printed caption. Lacy decorative leaves, fibers, a hand-woven mat, leaf buttons and raffia photo corners dress up the page with texture and pattern.

TIME IN A BOTTLE
September/October 2000
Issue #20
Thelma Molkoski, Kakabeka Falls, Ontario, Canada

Rustic wooden pantry shelves literally preserve autumn memories cropped in jar shapes and tied up with country printed paper. Colorful pencil sketches fill shelf space with glass canning jars whose labels identify the time frame of the photos. A juicy red apple completes the edible theme.

FALL
September/October 2002
Issue #32
Andrea Steed, Rochester, Minnesota

Color prints mixed with black-and-whites lend visual interest to a simple, elegant layout unified with subtle leaf patterned paper. Extensive journaling explains the significance of the fall season from a young couple's perspective.

IDAHO
March/April 2001
Issue #23
Colleen Macdonald, Calgary, Alberta, Canada

Heavy with ripened grain, thousands of golden heads wave in the afternoon breeze, shimmering like ocean waves in the afternoon sun. These hand-drawn shafts provide close-up detail of the vast and expansive beauty of wheat fields ready for harvest. Tiny wheat heads pull the design element into the title as well.

DOUBLE OAK
September/October 2001
Issue #26
Cheryl Uribe, Grapevine, Texas

Perched on a crispy hay bale, two sisters pause during pumpkin-patch, farm-animal and hay-maze adventures for Mommy to snap a quick candid. Detailed journaling on a paper-cut fence gate fills in the remaining details of the autumn day outing. Inspired by the ranch logo, the jumbo-sized medallion includes two die-cut horses and a double-trunked tree filled with Texas-sized punched oak leaves.

A LOOK BACK: *Scrapbook Embellishments*

Today's cutting-edge products and adornments have enabled scrapbookers to move beyond one-dimensional pages into a brave new world of artistic expression. Embroidery floss, fibers, wire and beads can be creatively used to add the depth and texture needed to make pictures pop. Sequins, rhinestones, eyelets and charms add wonderful whimsy when accenting a page.

Embossing, stamping, punch art and die cuts have elevated the scrapbook page to an artist's canvas. The exponential growth of page embellishments, the striking and savvy creations resulting from their usage, coupled with the lack of risk these embellishments pose to your photos all but negates the question "Can I put that on my scrapbook page?"

WET MITTENS
Winter 1997
Issue #5
Lisa Garnett, Littleton, Colorado

Buttons and jute are used to create innovative mitten ties on this romp of a page. Inspired by a wooden sign created by the artist some years earlier, the use of sewing materials was cutting-edge when this page was first published.

September 3, 1997

Sammy's first day of Kindergarten. She was so excited to go to her new school. Her teacher is Mrs. Christensen (Mrs. C for short). She headed off to the afternoon class in her new pink dress, her Megara backpack & a beautiful bright smile!

FIRST DAY OF KINDERGARTEN
September/October 1998
Issue #8
Lisa Dixon, East Brunswick, New Jersey

A cross-stitched sampler makes a stunning frame for this off-to-school page. Stitching, whether to add a simple pattern and texture to pages, to indulge a homey quilted look or to attach beads, fibers or other embellishments, became increasingly popular over the years.

ROMANTIC WEEKEND

January/February 2002
Issue #28
Memory Makers
Photos Shelley Balzer, Bakersfield, California

Hearts punched from a strip of double-side mounting adhesive are adorned with tiny red glass marbles. The use of beads and marbles continues to gain popularity as scrapbookers recognize their bold and passionate appeal.

SUNFLOWER

September/October 2002
Issue #32
Andrea Hautala, Olympia, Washington

Fiber plays a key role in the creation of this powerful sunflower embellishment. A circle punched from brown paper is adorned with yellow fuzzy fiber. Multiple strands of fibers are twisted for the stem and woven through the title. The use of fibers, whether jute, ribbon, floss, thread or yarn helped open up new design horizons for modern scrapbookers.

TIMELESS

January/February 2003
Issue #34
Torrey Miller, Thornton, Colorado

Interactive pages including this timeless beauty are easy to make with the wide range of products which became available as scrapbook pages began to be mobile. By spinning the wheel, new pictures are revealed. Additional embellishments of charms, buttons, ribbon, embroidery floss, punches and stickers make taking a trip back down Memory Lane something to look forward to.

WINTER

"In winter we lead a more inward life. Our hearts are warm and cheery, like cottages under drifts, whose windows and doors are half concealed, but from whose chimneys the smoke cheerfully ascends," wrote Henry David Thoreau, a 19th-century American philosopher.

His insight still applies to modern-day scrapbookers who, in the welcoming coziness of homes and cropping circles, chronicle warm memories of even the coldest winter moments.

WINTER WONDERLAND
January/February 2003
Issue #34
Kenna Ewing, Parkside, Pennsylvania

A red photo mat, tall border strips and template-cut title letters warm up a thoughtful winter page. Polka-dot paper that suggests softly falling snow and a photo-quality border strip of lacy white trees expand the background of the pensive winter portrait.

PSALMS 42:1
January/February 2000
Issue #16
Pamela Zenger, Spokane, Washington

Bold die cuts give fullness to a snowflake wreath woven with curving, cream-colored vines. Against a softly patterned background, smaller snowflakes, punched and layered, develop a lacy effect to complement the jagged edges of the wandering winter stream.

CATHEDRAL ARCHES
Holiday/Winter 1997
Issue #5
Memory Makers
Photos Erica Pierovich, Longmont, Colorado

A silhouetted frame offers a view of a winter panorama complete with deer, mountains and whirling snowflakes. A dark frame coupled with a collage of photos and printed papers create a glowing, surreal stained-glass window.

BLANKET OF SNOW
January/February 2003
Issue #34
Debbie Mock, Denver, Colorado

With edges wrapped in silver thread, deep navy paper sets off filigreed photos of snowy winter trees. Patterned paper stirs memories of the swirling storm that bequeathed a dazzling white blanket.

SLIP 'N SLIDE
January/February 2002
Issue #28
Teri Cutts, Portland, Oregon

A color-blocked background covered with printed vellum, snowflakes and letters textured with tiny clear marbles, and hand-stitched accents bring crisp creativity to a winter wonderland slide show. The blue color palette not only adds to the wintry feel but also ingeniously compensates for black-and-white photos that were printed a little too blue. Warm mittens with blanket-stitched edges and puffy flannel cuffs add a touch of cozy charm.

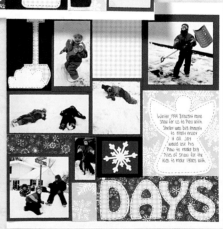

SNOWY DAYS
November/December 1999
Issue #15
Dorothy Ferreira, Woodcliff Lake, New Jersey

As cozy as a homemade quilt, this snowy day spread incorporates square cropped photos and blocks of coordinating patterned paper to piece together a comforting pattern. A freehand cut mug, mittens, snowman and other elements add charm, as does the pen "stitched" additions.

GENESEE MOUNTAIN
November/December 2001
Issue #27
Memory Makers

Saving brochures from a holiday tree sale made it easy to provide background information, maps and even illustrations for a snowy tree-cutting adventure. Photocopied onto vellum, the found elements blend well with the wintry patterned background paper and keep the focus on the three strong photographs.

WINTER HOW SWEET IT IS
January/February 2002
Issue #28
Tori Eaton, Springville, Utah

Sweet enough to rival chocolate? Yes! Young Adam's expression, captured in this animated photo, speaks louder than words. The simplicity of the page, embellished with letter stickers and a mini snowflake punch, supports the innocence of the age-old childhood pleasure of capturing elusive snowflakes on the tongue.

WINTER WONDERLAND
January/February 2003
Issue #34
Shauna Berglund-Immel, for Hot off the Press, Beaverton, Oregon

Beaded snowflake tags, eyelets, floss and ribbon work together to create a potent cool-weather page. Balance is what makes this layout work with larger embellishments coupled with more delicate decorative elements. The cool blues and patterned vellum support the loving photo.

SLEDDING
November/December 1999
Issue #15
Linda Crosby, Phoenix, Arizona

Frosty never looked so good as when featured in this fun and funny winter spread. Cropped photos form his body while freehand-cut arms and hat and punched eyes and mouth complete his person and define his personality. Layered papers, matted photos and the world's biggest cropped-photo snowflake round out the winter wonderland.

SKI BABIES
November/December 2002
Issue #33
Kelly Angard, Highlands Ranch, Colorado

Saved photo scraps contribute more elements to this fun ski page than the photos themselves. Scraps of faraway ski photos help fill each block-style letter. Scrap-punched snowflakes contrast well with the navy background. Even the little square accents that border the caption are recycled from snowy photo scraps.

SNOW FALLING ON CEDARS
January/February 2001
Issue #22
Michelle Kirby, Newton, North Carolina

Torn mulberry lends feathery edges to happy sledding photos set against a speckled navy background. The trees and letters illustrate the title with hand-cut mounds of snow.

A LOOK BACK: *Scrapbook Paper-Piecing*

Because paper has always been widely available to scrapbookers, paper-pieced designs have been a part of even the earliest creative scrapbook pages. Although in a sense every scrapbook page could be considered paper piecing, the term refers specifically to any cohesive design created with cut paper elements. The earliest examples were freehand cut and detailed with black pen.

New products including templates, stencils, patterns, books, computer software, paper-piecing kits, punches and die cuts now make it easy to create a paper replica of just about anything. Whether freehand cut or assembled from a peel-and-stick kit, paper piecing offers an appealing way to incorporate dimensional themes onto a flat surface.

SPRING
March/April 2002
Issue #29
Marianne Park, Cabot, Arkansas

Chalk-shaded, pen-detailed and jute-wrapped flowerpots hold bright spring blooms. The pattern-cut yellow daffodils with pale yellow petals and deep golden centers match the "Ice Follies" variety in the photos. Clip-art lettering shaded with colored pencils repeats the floral theme.

SHELL SEEKERS
September/October 1998
Issue #8
Leslie Graves, Pantego, Texas

Silhouette cropped and layered against a blue background, this beach home blends almost seamlessly with a paper-pieced second story that completes the picture. The layered paper design accurately reproduces the roof, windows, columns and other architectural details.

WILD ANIMAL PARK
July/August 2000
Issue #19
Terri Fusco, Claremont, California

A mosaic background randomly pieced from colored scraps creates a textured camouflage effect. In the foreground, a die-cut leaf border and a tall palm tree with a bright-eyed monkey further develop the jungle theme.

HAPPY HOME
September/October 1999
Issue #14
Vickie Mehallow, Troy, Illinois

Colored paper, colored pens and a bright grin are all it took to create this happy-go-lucky page. Elements, inspired by coloring book and storybook characters, are kicking up their heels with spirit that's infectious enough to make everyone want to join in the dance.

MAINE
May/June 2001
Issue #24
Christine Wallace, Steep Falls, Maine

A large state die cut forms the base for an intricate focal design pieced from both die-cut and hand-cut state icons. Photos in each corner, trimmed to silhouette the state outline and layered against solid and patterned papers, capture the natural beauty of Maine in all its seasonal glory.

THE BUS
September/October 2001
Issue #26
Donna Pittard, Kingwood, Texas

These school buses will stop for pedestrians, but they won't stop being appreciated any time soon. Freehand-cut yellow arches, silver bumpers and black wheels are pieced together to form photo frames which embrace goin'-off-to-school adventure. Letter stickers and printed paper add even more zip to the scene.

POINSETTIAS
November/December 2000
Issue #21
Susan Walker, Oakbrook Terrace, Illinois

Raised edges add a finishing touch to each section of these elegant poinsettias. Cut using a stencil and outlined with an embossing stylus, the designs pieced from rich reds, greens and golds echo the colors of Christmas as well as the simply cropped and captioned photos.

CONCORDIA LUTHERAN CHURCH
November/December 2000
Issue #21
Memory Makers

Simply torn and layered from solid and vellum paper, a whimsical angel smiles at young Sunday-school singers. Music notes and a star seem to float above in a starry green sky. Torn and pieced strips frame the page with color and pattern.

SPRING

Author Virgil A. Kraft wrote, "Spring shows what God can do with a drab and dirty world." Likewise, spring pages show what scrapbookers can do when inspired by nature's annual redecorating. Pages that burst with flowers, foliage, fresh air and blue sky reflect the hope and joy of this renewal.

FIELD OF BEAUTY

July/August 2002
Issue #31
Pamela Frye, Denver, Colorado
Photos Chrissie Tepe, Lancaster, California

Borders of embossed confetti mirror the brilliant colors in poppy-field photos arranged in a balanced checkerboard design. The square title, caption and smaller photo further reinforce this symmetry. Contemporary letter stickers write an appropriate title.

GOD'S HEART

May/June 1999
Issue #12
Lisa Laird, Orange City, Iowa

Daylilies, roses, pansies, sunflowers, daisies, bleeding hearts, iris, asters, marigolds and zinnias are only a few of the bright varieties displayed on a quilted layout stitched with a thin pink pen. Uniform heart shapes provide consistency and balance, allowing the vivid color to effectively frame a poetic sentiment.

OUR HOUSE
March/April 2001
Issue #23
Chris Peters, Hasbrouck Heights, New Jersey

Flourishing foliage and vivid spring blossoms are always a visual delight, especially in this careful arrangement of 1" mosaic squares. The design gives the illusion of looking at a lush garden through a many-paned window. Pale sage mats against the evergreen background bring focus to the heartfelt caption and house photo.

BUCHART GARDENS
July/August 2001
Issue #25
Cori Dahmen, for Me and My BIG Ideas, Lake Forest, California

Tied to the caption and affixed to the page edges with flower stickers, sheer pink ribbon adds a shimmering accent to richly colored garden photos. Colorful floral stickers fill in blooming title letters and add detail to corner embellishments.

SPRING
SUN, MARCH WIND
March/April 2000
Issue #17
Lois Carpenter, Bayfield, Colorado

Curtains tickle. Just ask Wesley, who shared the pleasures of a warm spring breeze with these drapes. Creamy colors and punched swirls frame this airy page. A freehand-cut cloud serves as a journaling block. Six small clouds are layered to form the wind's body while the rush of air he emits is freehand cut.

SPRING HAS SPRUNG
March/April 2002
Issue #29
Memory Makers
Photo Tina Heine, Carrollton, Georgia

Because of its literal flexibility, wire is a versatile material that is both easy and fun to bend, twist, wrap, coil, curl, bead and shape into uniquely entertaining page embellishments. In this well-wired page, a variety of colors and gauges frame four giggling girls with texture and dimension. Coiled title letters make the title a witty play on words.

SWEETNESS OF SPRING
March/April 2001
Issue #23
Sharon Kropp, Paonia, Colorado

Artist-designed dotted script lettering on a softly curved banner heralds charming spring photos. The style ties in the polka dots in the blue, pink and floral papers. Vellum frames that overlay the matted photos soften the edges as well as accentuate winsome smiles.

GARDEN OF MY DREAMS
May/June 2003
Issue #36

Kelly Angard, Highlands Ranch, Colorado
Photos Denise Stuesse, Sammamish, Washington

It has been said that blueprints are future dreams laid down on paper. Dreams of a perfect garden became the reality of a perfect scrapbook spread for Kelly. A photocopy of a garden blueprint, floral photos, vellum and penwork bloomed into a joyful explosion of spring color.

DESTINATIONS
May/June 2003
Issue #36

Jane Rife, Hendersonville, Tennessee

Everyone needs a quiet place, a gentle place, a place to heal and a place to dream. This garden is that and more. A brilliant floral border grounds the page. Other elements float on creamy daffodil colored paper. A substantial journaling block and a single photo add balance and warmth to this layout, like a well-planned garden on a gentle afternoon.

FRESH CALIFORNIA LEMONADE
July/August 2001
Issue #25
Memory Makers
Photos Charlotte Wilhite, Arlington, Texas

One-two-three...forget saying "cheese" and just pucker for the camera. A spring day collecting lemons for lemonade is honored on a lemon lime woven background that screams "citrus." Add a cup of sugar and you've got a page that's sweet as can be.

SKY HIGH
March/April 2001
Issue #23
Pennie Stutzman, Broomfield, Colorado

Created with duplicate panoramic photos mounted in opposite directions, a billowing, funnel-shaped spiral conveys the drama and movement associated with an exciting aerial adventure. Two adjacent photo panels dial up the intensity with saturated balloon colors, while elongated lettering mimics flying flags in a patchy blue sky. A photo pocket behind the left page holds a detailed, pull-out caption.

TRIPLE PLAY
March/April 2003
Issue #35
Deb Clover, St. Michael, Minnesota

An eyelet-studded, hand-stitched baseball glove replicates the well-worn gear that caught the first out in a memorable triple play. The color photo sequence breaks down the lightning-fast moment so the reader can feel the action. Sepia-toned photos, printed using an "antique" setting, heighten the drama with an interesting bird's-eye view. A detailed caption and baseball title lettering tell the exciting story.

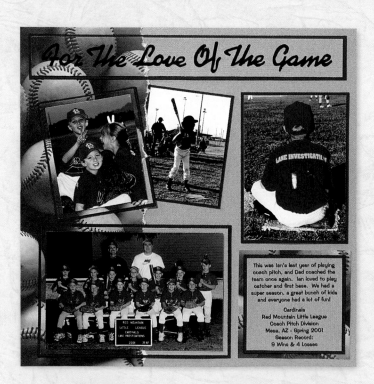

FOR THE LOVE OF THE GAME
July/August 2002
Issue #31
Beth Rogers, Mesa, Arizona

Printed baseball paper makes a torn background and mat that can't strike out. In fact, this whole page is something to cheer about. Bright red mats coordinate with team jerseys and pop against the light brown paper. Whether in the outfield or on the diamond, this page is a jewel.

MY WEEKEND WARRIOR
May/June 2003
Issue #36
Jane Rife, Hendersonville, Tennessee

Yardwork calls and Jane's husband is up for the task. Photos of him tending to business are mounted on handmade paper embellished with stamped leaves. Mesh, fiber and eyelets add an earthy, organic feel to this outdoor page.

A LOOK BACK: *Quilted Scrapbook Pages*

Although quilters use fabric, batting, needles and thread, while scrapbookers use photos, paper, adhesive and pen stitching, both combine their materials into a collage of color, pattern and texture, carefully pieced to last generations. Because quilted pages require only photos, paper and a black pen, they have been a popular design technique from the earliest days of creative scrapbooking. *Memory Makers Quilted Scrapbooks*, published in 2000, compiles hundreds of quilt designs in a delightful, inspiring book that includes simple patchwork pages as well as more complex piecings.

Today's scrapbook market also offers specialized tools and templates that make page quilting even easier. Because the variations of any design are infinite, the beauty of scrapbook quilts is that no two designs turn out quite the same. Scrapbook quilts, like their cozy counterparts, wrap readers in the warmth and memory of friends, family and traditions.

HEARTS AND VINES
Spring 1998
Issue #6
Marilyn Garner, San Diego, California

A paper-punched garland of evergreen leaves and bright red berries frames a 12-heart quilt block filled with flowers, swirls and sweethearts. Simple pen stitching adds homespun detail.

FRESH FLOWERS
March/April 1999
Issue #11
Marilyn Garner, San Diego, Calfornia

Dry-embossed quilted designs come to light with thin pen-stitched outlines. With circle-cropped centers and pale green leaves, plump lavender flowers balance the dimensional mauve squares. A wavy stitched border fluidly hems the design.

SEASONS
January/February 2001
Issue #22
Melody Sperl, Fairborn, Ohio

Beautifully penned Joni Mitchell lyrics border a kaleidoscope quilt that weaves a circle with geometric stick figures and paper hearts. The lines and angles pull the eye both inward to the central photo and outward to the color-blocked border and lacy calligraphy. The muted colors convey a quiet and peaceful tone.

CHRISTMAS PATCHWORK
Winter 1997
Issue #5
Marilyn Garner, San Diego, California

Christmas programs, family gatherings and holiday smiles blend easily in this appliqué quilt. Traced from a book of quilting patterns, each folk-art shape represents a familiar Christmas icon. Red sashing strips and green corner squares unite the figures in a cohesive patchwork design.

POINSETTIA GARLAND
November/December 2002
Issue #33
Donna Pittard, Kingwood, Texas

The detailed appliqués of Baltimore Album quilts inspired this punch-art reproduction crafted with a large circle, small heart, poinsettia and mini flower punches. The scalloped border provides a festive, lacy look to four square-cropped Christmas photos. The tan edges trimmed with pinking scissors and layered over patterned paper create the illusion of blanket stitching.

ILLUSTRATED GLOSSARY OF SCRAPBOOK TERMS AND TECHNIQUES

Modern scrapbooking evolved from a growing concern that products used in putting together memory albums were actually damaging, rather than preserving, both photos and memorabilia. One of the biggest culprits in the deterioration of photos was "magnetic albums" which gained popularity in the 70s. These convenient memory books allow scrapbookers to place their photos and memorabilia on sticky pages and cover them with an attached sheet of transparent plastic. Too late, it was discovered that the PVC coupled with adhesive and acidic papers create a "sandwich of death" which causes photos to yellow and become brittle. The need for higher quality scrapbooking products was apparent. Examples of safer products were found in memory books displayed at the 1980 World Conference on Records. These albums, created by members of the Mormon community, sparked an increased public interest in safe photo archiving. Creative Memories, a scrapbooking company founded in the late 1980s, spread the word about safe versus unsafe products as well as selling supplies and tools. In subsequent years, the craft's popularity grew. Scrapbooking and hobby stores clamored for supplies and tools. Manufacturers answered the cry. Eventually a vocabulary developed surrounding supplies, concerns and scrapbooking techniques which testifies to the commitment of scrapbookers and industry professionals to eradicate the mistakes of the past in order to preserve what is precious to us for the future.

ACCESSORIES
Page accents that you make or buy. Can include stickers, die cuts, stamped images and punch art. May also include baubles (beads, buttons, rhinestones, sequins), colorants (pens, chalk, inkpads), metallics (charms, wire, jewelry-making components, eyelets, fasteners), textiles (ribbon, embroidery floss, thread), or organics (raffia, pressed flowers and leaves, tiny shells, sand). While one-dimensional accessories traditionally adorned scrapbook pages, there now exists a limitless array of cutting-edge and even three-dimensional products that may be safely used on scrapbook pages.

ACID-FREE
Although acids were once prevalent in photo album papers and products, the damage caused by acids to photographs and memorabilia has been realized and should be avoided. Look for scrapbook products—particularly pages, paper, adhesives and inks—that are free from destructive acids that can eat away at the emulsion on your photos. Harmful acids can occur in the manufacturing process. Check labels for "acid-free" and "photo-safe."

ADHESIVES
A far departure from the gloppy glues of the past, modern adhesives come in both "wet" and "dry" applications depending on one's needs and are used to adhere or attach photos, accessories and memorabilia to scrapbook pages. Buy and use only acid-free and photo-safe adhesives in a scrapbook to dramatically extend the life of your photos and scrapbook materials.

ALBUM
The archival-quality book in which you place your finished scrapbook pages for posterity and for safekeeping. Available in a number of shapes and sizes, albums may be secure pages in post-bound, binder, spiral or strap-hinge style. Archival albums should be purchased in place of the previously popular magnetic albums, which can destroy photos and memorabilia; remove items and place in safer albums.

ARCHIVAL QUALITY
A nontechnical term suggesting that a substance is chemically stable, durable and permanent. This distinction suggests superior quality and low-risk for adverse effects to photography and memorabilia.

BORDER
The upper, lower and side edges or margins of a scrapbook page. Sometimes refers to a border design that is handmade or manufactured and attached to a page.

BUFFERED PAPER
Paper in which certain alkaline substances have been added during the manufacturing process to prevent acids from forming in the future due to chemical reactions.

CARDSTOCK
The heaviest of scrapbook papers; can be solid colored or patterned. While also used for die cuts and pocket pages, many scrapbookers now look to the innumerable colors of cardstock to serve as pages.

CD-ROM
A compact disc that can store large amounts of digitized photos and data files. In scrapbooking, font and lettering CDs as well as scrapbook software CDs have become helpful tools in individually personalizing the page making process.

CROP
A term utilized by enthusiasts to describe an event attended by other scrapbookers for the purpose of scrapbooking, sharing ideas and tools and swapping products; held at conventions, craft and scrapbook stores, private homes, organized craft camps and crop-oriented vacations.

CROPPING
The act of cutting or trimming photos to enhance the image, eliminate unnecessary backgrounds or turn the photos into unique works of art. Whereas early albums most typically displayed photos in their entirety, safe and easy cropping tools have effectively undermined the notion that photographs should not be altered by means of cutting.

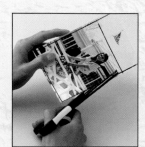

DE-ACIDIFY
To chemically treat paper memorabilia to neutralize acids while applying an alkaline buffer to discourage further acid migration from damaging photos.

DECORATIVE SCISSORS
While once pinking shears were a fancy departure from traditional straight-edge cutting, there now exists a multitude of scissors with special-cut blades or teeth that provide a wide array of cut patterns, designs and cutting depths. Flipping decorative scissors over will result in a varied cutting pattern.

DIE CUTS
Precut for purchase or self-cut paper shapes that come in both printed and solid colors. Decorative elements for adding a theme or accent to a page. Should be acid- and lignin-free.

DIGITAL
A computer-related term for the process of using numerical digits to create uniform photographic images as shot with a digital camera or scanned into a computer with a scanner and saved on and retrieved from a CD-ROM.

ENCAPSULATE
To encase paper or three-dimensional memorabilia in PVC-free plastic sleeves, envelopes and keepers for its own preservation and the protection of your photos.

JOURNALING
Refers to handwritten, handmade or computer-generated text that provides pertinent details about what is taking place in photographs.

LETTERING
The act of forming or creating letters to use in scrapbook page titles and journaling. Lettering can include freehand cut or drawn, sticker, die-cut, template-cut, stamped, punched letters or computer-generated letters.

LIGNIN-FREE
Paper and products that are void of the material (sap) that holds wood fibers together as a tree grows. Most paper is lignin-free except for newsprint, which yellows and becomes brittle with age. Check product labels to be on the safe side.

MATTING
The act of attaching paper, generally cropped in the shape of a photo, behind the photo to separate it from the scrapbook page's background paper.

MEMORABILIA
Mementos and souvenirs saved from travel, school and life's special events—things that are worthy of remembrance.

MOUNTING
The process of attaching photos or memorabilia to an album page. Permanent mounting requires the application of adhesive to the back of a photo or mat. Nonpermanent mounting allows you to attach your items to a page and still have the option of easily removing them.

ORGANIZATION
The act of putting together ordered photos and memorabilia for the purpose of scrapbooking. Organization of the scrapbook tools and supplies provides for maximum scrapbooking efficiency.

PAGE PROTECTORS
Plastic sleeves or pockets that encase finished scrapbook pages for protection. Use only PVC-free protectors.

PAGE TITLE
A general or descriptive heading put on a scrapbook page that sums up the theme or essence. Conversely, a "title page" is the first page at the front of a scrapbook, often decorated and embellished (without photos), that describes the book's content.

PHOTO-SAFE
A term used by companies to indicate that they feel their products are safe to use with photos in a scrapbook album.

PIGMENT INK
Pigment inks are water-insoluble and do not penetrate the paper surface. Instead, they adhere to the surface, providing better contrast and clarity. For journaling pens and inkpads, look for "acid-free" and "photo-safe" on the label.

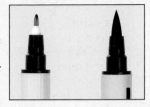

POCKET PAGE
A scrapbook page that has been transformed by the addition of a second sheet of cropped paper adhered to the surface, forming a "pocket" in which to place the paper memorabilia.

PRESERVATION
The act of stabilizing an item from deterioration through the use of proper methods and materials that maintain the conditions and longevity of the item.

PUNCHES
Tools in which paper is inserted and pressure is applied to produce particular shapes through a bladed configuration. Punches come in hundreds of sizes, shapes, designs, patterns, letters and numbers.

PVC OR POLYVINYL CHLORIDE
A plastic that should not be used in a scrapbook, it emits gases that cause damage to photos. Use only PVC-free plastic page protectors and memorabilia keepers. Safe plastics include polypropylene, polyethylene and polyester.

SHAPE CUTTERS
Shape cutters are bladed tools that are useful for cropping photos, mats and journaling blocks into perfect shapes. They can cut in circles, ovals and many other simple shapes.

STAMPS
A wood and rubber tool used to impress a design on paper or cloth; used with a stamp pad or inkpad. With just a few stamps and an inkpad, you can make delicate borders, lacy photo corners, stamped backgrounds, eye-catching photo mats, dressed-up die cuts and jazzy page accents.

STICKERS
Gummed with adhesive on one side and a design or pattern on the other, stickers are one of the easiest ways to embellish scrapbook pages. There are thousands of designs to choose from in a multitude of colors, themes and styles—including letter and number, border, journaling and design element stickers.

TEMPLATES
Templates are stencil-like patterns made of plastic, sturdy paper or cardboard. They can be homemade or purchased and can be used for creating letters, shapes, page borders, and journaling guides. Nested templates are transparent and have cutting channels for blades to travel along to cut paper and photographs into desired shapes.

INDEX